Spider
Woman's
Web

Spider Woman's Web

Traditional
Native American Tales
About
Women's Power

SUSAN HAZEN-HAMMOND

A Perigee Book

A Perigee Book
Published by The Berkley Publishing Group
A division of Penguin Putnam Inc.
375 Hudson Street
New York, New York 10014

First edition: November 1999

Published simultaneously in Canada.

The Penguin Putnam Inc. World Wide Web site address is
www.penguinputnam.com

Library of Congress Cataloging-in-Publication Data

Hazen-Hammond, Susan.
Spider woman's web : traditional Native American tales about
women's power / Susan Hazen-Hammond. — 1st ed.
p. cm.
Includes bibliographical references and index.
ISBN 0-399-52546-7
1. Indians of North America—Folklore. 2. Women—Folklore. 3. Tales—North
America. I. Title.
E98.F6 H545 1999
398.2'089'97—dc21   99-35823
CIP

Printed in the United States of America

20 19 18 17 16 15

"All tales are born in the mind of Spider Woman,
and all tales exist as a result of her naming."

—PAULA GUNN ALLEN,
The Sacred Hoop, 1991

This book is dedicated to all Native American storytellers,
living and deceased, who have kept tribal stories alive since
the days, long ago, when the world was a small island, ruled
by a woman who was a giant.

Contents

Introduction

E ver since the first human beings sat around the first campfires at night, they have told stories. Turning their backs to the darkness, people stared at the flames, breathed the smoke, and listened to the truth-sayers of their place and time tell stories that entertained them, taught them, and spoke to the unconscious.

In the Americas, this tradition has continued into the present, creating one of the oldest surviving bodies of literature on earth. Some Native American stories may have been repeated a million times, across a thousand generations or more. In simple, straightforward language, they speak of the core components of human life: death, birth, love, hate, grief, happiness, anxiety, courage, calm—the same issues that psychologists, psychiatrists, and other therapists explore.

Even just looking at the part of the Americas that is today the United States, Native America was never a single culture, but always a multitude of cultures, traditions, viewpoints, values, languages, and heritages. Still, as Paula Gunn Allen and numerous other scholars have pointed out, the tendency across the continent was toward appreciating, honoring, and even worshipping the powers of women.

Through the centuries, while their counterparts in Europe grew up on stories that depicted women as weak, helpless, sinister, or untrustworthy, Native American women grew up hearing tales about the powers and strengths of women. They heard stories about women healers, women warriors, women artists, women prophets. But above all, they heard stories of woman as the divine creator, woman as a supernatural power, woman as a force of transformation in the universe.

There are dozens of variations in the details, but the core meaning is consistent: women, and the female forces of the universe, are strong. Sometimes they are so powerful that they can change the course of the world. Often, once they take a stand, they change their own lives and the lives of those around them.

Like good stories everywhere, Native American tales contain literal truths and symbolic truths, along with layers of meaning that go as deep as the mind of the listener can go, and deeper. Like some rare hybrid that combines the bloodiest action-adventure movies with the loftiest prize-winning literature, they include the full range of human behavior, from the wisest and noblest to the most horrifying.

There is no family so dysfunctional that it hasn't already starred in a Native American legend. There is no relationship or human dynamic so brutal that some Native American story hasn't already covered it: murder, rape, arson, torture, betrayal, child abuse, incest, violence of every sort.

It's all here, from cannibalism to virgin births.

One aspect of oral tradition is that the story changes, sometimes slightly, sometimes significantly, from storyteller to storyteller and generation to generation. In working with storytellers among the Navajo and among the Tohono O'odham of southern Arizona, I have observed this firsthand. One day, while I was sitting on the desert floor in the shade of a mesquite tree with Regina Siquieros, a prominent Tohono O'odham storyteller, she explained, "Sometimes the details change each time I tell a story. And I know other storytellers tell these stories in different ways. Even my sister and I don't tell the same story exactly the same way. But the underlying meaning remains. And each time we tell these stories, they reconnect us and our listeners to our ancestors and our roots."

All the stories presented here have been modified through the centuries, and there's no way we can know exactly what they were like five hundred years ago. In addition, just as two people looking at the same painting will see different things, so two people hearing or reading the same story will focus on different details. This is particularly true when stories from one culture are viewed through the filter of another.

Following the long-standing practice of oral tradition, I have retold the stories and songs presented here in my own words, always striving to retain the core meaning. In selecting stories from the thousands that have been recorded in the past two hundred years, I have emphasized those that best portray the power, strength, and vitality of women. As much as possible, I have chosen to follow the most traditional and most conservative versions of these tales, often from stories first written down generations ago.

The stories also represent a rough cross-section of tribes and regions from around the country. A system of icons, first developed for my book *Timelines of Native American History*, reappears here, so that readers interested in following the traditions of certain regions of the country can find them quickly.

A century ago, Zitkala-Sa, a Dakota (Sioux) storyteller, wrote down the stories of her people. In 1902, in the introduction to *Old Indian Legends*, she said, "The old legends of America belong quite as much to the blue-eyed little patriot as to the black-haired aborigine." She believed that in sharing these tales with non-Indians, she was giving people a chance to see the common themes that link all humans everywhere.

Part of the power of Native American stories is that they combine ordinary elements from everyday life with images, symbols, and themes from the unconscious. Like dreams, they make us take another look at ourselves and our lives. Full of nuance and complexity, they contain symbols that are universal. They speak to us from across the eons. They give us a mirror in which to see ourselves.

These stories are the seeds, and we are the ground in which their messages grow.

The stories presented here stand by themselves. Just reading them is enough to jar things loose inside us. However, because some readers may want a framework around which to weave the strands of their own inner explorations, questions and suggestions accompany each story. Following my own belief that there is seldom one right way of doing things or one right way of looking at the world, they relate to many ways of thinking and many schools of psychology. The one underlying assumption is that all human beings yearn, in varying degrees, and with varying levels of awareness, for completeness and wholeness, that all of us long to be the person we are meant to be, the person we are capable of being.

For those who wish to use them, the exercises, or "Connections," as I prefer to call them, provide tools to help in your quest for deeper meaning and a stronger sense of self. They may shine light on areas within you that you have previously overlooked. They may make it easier to complete your life's task of becoming more fully who you are.

They will also help you take inventory of your life. Depending on what point you are at in your own personal journey, they may stimulate you to embark on a full-blown life review.

Rather than parse each story exhaustively, I have selected half a dozen features from each to serve as a springboard for thought about our own lives and hearts. These stories are so rich in symbols that it would take several volumes to explore them all. But certain images, symbols, and themes recur like leitmotifs from one story to the next; by the end of the book, you will have used many of these in examining your own life.

Remember that you are the best judge of what is best for you. Use whichever exercises are most meaningful to you. Ignore any that don't resonate for you. Spend extra time on those to which you find yourself having some particularly strong response, either positive or negative.

In order to get the most out of the questions and suggestions, you may wish to do the following:

1. As you read the stories and do the Connections exercises, pay close attention to memories, feelings, associations, dreams. Write these down.

2. If you don't already keep a journal, or if you would like to keep a separate journal as you go through this book, buy a beautiful notebook or blank book, something so pretty or striking that it makes your heart sing. You may also want a separate looseleaf binder to store other papers in, and some pocket- or purse-sized notebooks to jot down ideas, emotions, and associations that come to you throughout the day.

3. If you prefer not to write, record your thoughts on tape. These tapes are just for you. No one else need ever hear them. (By all means allow your inner teenager free rein to post Do Not Disturb signs, or devise ways to store the tapes and journal where they won't be disturbed by others.) Another effective approach, augmenting or bypassing both journals and tapes, is to read the stories with a friend, then discuss your thoughts and reactions and the associations the story produces.

4. Clear a small corner of one room to make a shrine or meditation table: a place where you can arrange displays that honor yourself and your process. This can be modest: a small table, a dresser top, any area that you can claim as yours and decorate as you wish. You may want to cover it with a particularly pretty cloth or one that has been handed down through your family from a woman to whom you feel some special connection.

5. Find a quiet place that can be your place of solitude, your place of healing, as you go through this book. It should be a place

where you can meditate, do visualizations, write, paint, or simply sit and let your mind drift without being interrupted or distracted.

6. If you enjoy art projects, buy a portfolio carrier to store any artworks you make. If you don't already have basic art supplies, wander through a crafts store or art supply store and pick up paints in whatever colors and media that most appeal to you, along with appropriate art pads, drawing pads, etc.

7. Before you read further, meditate quietly for a few minutes. Or simply let your mind drift. Or sit with eyes closed and observe your breath flowing in and out.

   You might also use a technique borrowed from the Navajo tradition. Go outside and find a spiderweb. Sit beside it. Let your eyes wander up and down its intricate connections. Cut your mind loose from the day-to-day world and let it float with the web as it waves back and forth on the breeze. Feel the wind caress your skin. Perhaps it is Messenger Wind, sent from Spider Woman herself, to give you some wise insight before you begin.

Whatever approach you choose in going through this book, the key is to follow your intuition and select the method that is right for you. Even if you don't like to analyze or wouldn't dream of sharing your most personal thoughts with your friends, the very act of allowing yourself to think about these stories can lead to a step—or many steps—along the road to wholeness.

As you work through the Connections exercises, remember that the only wrong answer is one in which you are dishonest with yourself. Consider, too, that whatever work you produce is a gift to your future self. It's also a way of preserving the present and honoring the past.

Above all, approach the stories with reverence and respect. They come from the Ancestors. We are the instruments for preserving them for those who are not yet born.

This book is meant not to create gaps between men and women, but to heal them. It is written in the spirit of Spider Woman, whose many powers include the ability to restore harmony to humankind. It is written in the hope that we may all know the courage, wisdom, and love of White Star Woman. May we all, in our hearts, inhabit White Star Woman's garden, where the flowers are always blooming and the grass is always green.

KEY TO SYMBOLS

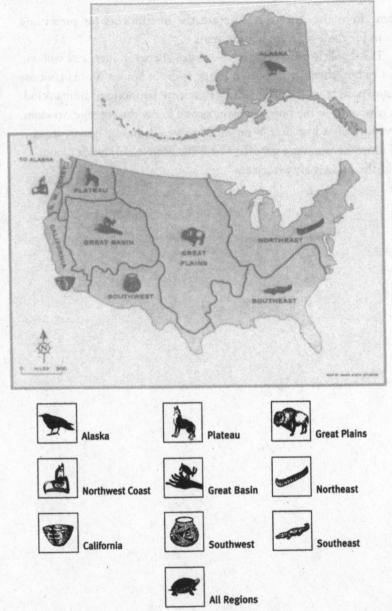

The symbols above appear throughout this book to indicate in which region or regions of the country each of the events occurred.

Chapter One

Spider Woman Saves
Ko-chin-ni-na-ko

A Tale from the Keresan Pueblos

This story, from the Keresan-speaking Pueblo peoples of New Mexico, combines elements of many genres of fiction: horror, murder mystery, mainstream, science fiction, romance. Like the best stories from cultures around the world, it makes us ask questions: What causes us to make mistakes? How can we undo them? What are our core strengths—and core weaknesses? It also introduces us to three images of women:

- the bewildered mother

- the innocent woman whose naïve trust may cause her destruction

- the wise woman whose understanding of the world is so complete that she can do things that for others would be impossible

This wise woman appears in several forms: as Spider Woman herself, as the Spirit of Memory, and as the Spirit of Reason.

Finally, in the person of Masts-tru-oi, we see the brutal effects of denial, and of expecting other people to meet our needs.

Few people are as blatantly evil as Masts-tru-oi, and probably no living person is as wise or as powerful as Spider Woman.

As you read this story, you will probably find that it triggers thoughts, memories, and feelings related to your own life and experiences, and to the lives and experiences of those you know and love. For most people, these associations flit in and out of consciousness quickly. You may want to read with journal or notebook in hand, jotting down key words or phrases that will help you recall these associations later.

Long ago a woman gave birth to a son, whom she named Masts-tru-oi. They lived on a ledge halfway up an enormous cliff face. Below them lay the plains. Above them, on the top of the cliff, grew the trees. There was only one way to reach the ledge, on a secret and dangerous path across the face of the cliff.

Masts-tru-oi grew up to be handsome and charming. But in spite of his mother's kindness and love, he developed a terrible temper. An insatiable longing grew inside him to find the perfect woman, someone who would meet all his needs, someone he would never grow tired of.

One day Masts-tru-oi traveled down the secret path that led to the base of the cliff and wandered across the plains to a nearby settlement. There he selected the most beautiful, most pleasant woman he could find to be his wife. But when he brought her home, he tired of her quickly.

One day, in a rage, while his wife was grinding corn, he grabbed her by her long black hair and threw her off the cliff as casually as if she had been a dried-out corncob.

Before her bones were bare, he climbed down the cliff again and traveled to another settlement. There he selected another wife, even more pleasant and more beautiful than the one he had married before. But he grew tired of her quickly, too. And he threw her off the cliff.

Soon it became a habit. If a woman refused him, as he searched the settlements for yet another wife, he simply kidnapped her and ruled her in terror until he grew bored. Then her bones joined the bones of her predecessors, far below the cliffside home.

At first, Masts-tru-oi's mother pretended she didn't see what was going on. Finally she could pretend no more, and tried to reason with her son. But nothing she said could dissuade him, and he was too big and too strong for her to use force. One day he threatened to throw her off, too, if she interfered with him in any way. From that day on, she stopped hearing and seeing, and she moved like a dead person through her days.

One day in his wanderings, as he searched for the perfect wife, Masts-tru-oi arrived at the village of Kush Kut-ret, on the banks of the great river. There he met Ko-chin-ni-na-ko, the oldest daughter of the headman. Using all his charms, Masts-tru-oi convinced her to become his wife. Although her mother and her father and her sisters were sorry to see her leave, Masts-tru-oi had deceived everyone so well that even her family approved of her marriage.

At first, Masts-tru-oi was happy to have the daughter of such an important man as his wife. But before long he felt himself growing tired of even her.

One morning he took her to a part of the cliff dwelling she had never seen before. There he showed her a storage room overflowing with cobs of blue corn.

"My wife," he said, "you must prove that you love me by shelling and grinding all the corn in this room before I return home tonight."

Then he went off, as he did every day, to visit his friend, the Spirit of the Storm, who lived by the side of the sea.

Her husband's strange request frightened Ko-chin-ni-na-ko. Although she was very industrious, and could grind corn faster than anyone else in her village, she knew it would be impossible to shell and grind so much corn in a single day.

Ko-chin-ni-na-ko sat on some corncobs and cried.

"Sister, why are you crying?" a voice asked.

It was Spider Old Woman.

Ko-chin-ni-na-ko explained her problem. "My husband has a terrible temper," she said. "I'm afraid if I don't please him, he will throw me off the cliff."

"Sister, do not cry," Spider Woman said. "Wait here for me to come back, and I will help you."

When Spider Woman returned, a flock of magic turkeys waddled behind her. Together Ko-chin-ni-na-ko and Spider Woman shelled the corn. Then the magic turkeys ground it. The birds worked so fast that soon the smell of ground corn hung heavy in the air.

By midafternoon the bare cobs lay in a heap, and the blue corn, ground into fine blue meal, rose in a pile beside it.

That night Masts-tru-oi came home in a happy mood. "So, have you finished grinding all that corn?" he asked playfully, as he imagined himself picking this boring woman up and tossing her to her death, just as he had done to his other wives.

Ko-chin-ni-na-ko led her husband to the room.

"Well," he said angrily when he saw the pile of finely ground corn, "don't think that ends your work." He led her to another room, jammed to the ceiling with cobs of red corn.

The next day, Spider Woman and the magic turkeys helped Ko-chin-ni-na-ko again. Long before the sun went down, the two women had finished rubbing the red kernels off the cobs, and the turkeys had finished grinding them. A heap of red cornmeal rose to the ceiling.

Again Masts-tru-oi raged. Again, he took his wife to another room, this one full of white corn, and ordered her to grind it before he returned home.

Again Spider Woman and the magic turkeys saved Ko-chin-ni-na-ko.

On the fourth day, they ground a roomful of multicolored corn.

Masts-tru-oi was more annoyed than ever.

"Tomorrow you must travel far to the north, to the other side of the mountains, and bring me back a jar of water from the White Lake," he said. "If you don't return by evening, that proves you're a bad wife. And I will throw you off the cliff."

"But I have heard that the path crosses rugged mountains," Ko-chin-ni-na-ko said. "And even if that is not true, it is too far to walk in one day."

Masts-tru-oi just laughed. Ko-chin-ni-na-ko cried.

But the more she cried, the harder her husband laughed. He rolled over and went to sleep, and dreamed of the pleasure he would have in throwing her off the cliff because she had failed him as a wife. Then he could set out again and resume his search for the perfect wife.

The next morning, he woke up happy and went off to have a good time with his friend, the Spirit of the Storm. Ko-chin-ni-na-ko balanced a jar on her head and set out northward, toward the mountains that are the home of the White Lake. It was better to die trying to reach the lake, she decided, than to have her husband fling her off the cliff.

After traveling many hours, she sat down to rest. The mountains looked as far away as they had when she first set out.

"Where are you going, sister?" a voice asked. It was Spider Old Woman.

Ko-chin-ni-na-ko told her all that had happened.

"There is no way you can reach the White Lake," Spider Woman said. "Sit here and watch the mountains. I will help you."

Ko-chin-ni-na-ko sat, and as she watched, the mountains grew larger and larger, until the White Lake came into view. Soon it lay so close that the water lapped against her toes. She knelt down and filled the jar. Then, thanking Spider Woman once more, she put it on her head and started home.

Long before her husband's return, she reached their ledge house and set the jar of water in the middle of the room.

When Masts-tru-oi tasted it, he said, "Yes, this is water from the White Lake. But this is not enough. It does not prove anything. You are not a good wife. Tomorrow you must prove your worth by bringing water from the Blue Lake."

"But the Blue Lake is even farther than the White Lake. And they say the path is impassable," Ko-chin-ni-na-ko said.

Although she cried and begged, her husband ignored her. "Remember what will happen, if you fail," he said.

The next day as she was walking toward the Blue Lake, Spider Old Woman saw her. "Where are you going, sister?" she asked.

"To the Blue Lake," Ko-chin-ni-na-ko said.

"You could never reach it," Spider Woman replied. "But this time I cannot bring it to you, because tomorrow your husband will follow your trail. Give me your jar and your shoes. I will bring the water."

That night Masts-tru-oi grew so angry when he saw the water from the Blue Lake that Ko-chin-ni-na-ko thought he was going to kill her right then. Instead, he said, "You are a terrible wife, the worst I have ever had. You are evil. You are a witch. I am going away for four days. That should give you time enough to realize how terrible you are. If you have not died of shame by the time I return, then I will throw you off the cliff." He dragged her by her hair to the edge of the cliff and pushed her head down. In the moonlight, she could see the white bones of all the wives who had preceded her, scattered across the plains.

She wanted to run away, but she was frightened. After her husband left, she sat and sobbed until she thought she would die crying.

"Why are you crying, sister?" the voice of Spider Woman asked.

When Ko-chin-ni-na-ka told her, Spider Woman said, "Do not be afraid. Wait here, and on the third day I will return."

Spider Woman went home and spun a silk thread so long that she could roll it up in a giant ball.

On the third day, she went back to get Ko-chin-ni-na-ko and led the young woman to a hidden place on the face of the cliff. Then she handed her the end of the ball of webbing.

"Whatever you do, don't look back up at me until you reach the ground," Spider Woman said. "If you do, the cord will break, and you will fall as surely to your death as if your husband had thrown you off the cliff like all his other wives."

Ko-chin-ni-na-ko clutched the silk thread and looked down at the ground far below. She felt dizzy and sick, but she knew she had no choice. Without looking back once, she descended to the ground and hurried off in the direction of her father's village.

All morning she walked eastward, and all afternoon, until the light slanted low across the plains from the west, warming her back.

Without warning, night fell all at once.

Behind her, enormous black clouds swirled in the sky, completely blocking the day's last light. It was Masts-tru-oi and his friend, the Spirit of the Storm, chasing her.

All across the plains, there was no place to hide.

"Ko-chin-ni-na-ko," a voice called.

She looked up. Spider Old Woman stood nearby.

"Let's go to my house," said Spider Woman. "You'll be safe there."

But when they reached Spider Woman's house, Ko-chin-ni-na-ko saw that it was too small for her to enter.

The black clouds were so close that she could see her husband riding them, side by side with his friend, the Spirit of the Storm. Fury twisted Masts-tru-oi's face so that it looked like a mask.

The Spirit of the Storm spoke in thunder so loud that the far mountains trembled and the cliffs shook.

"Just put your foot in the door of my house," Spider Woman urged.

Ko-chin-ni-na-ko did, and instantly the house expanded until it was large enough for her to enter.

Rain dropped in sheets from the sky, and hail pounded the earth like rocks. Lightning flashed from all sides, striking Spider Woman's home over and over. But inside, Spider Woman and Ko-chin-ni-na-ko stayed warm, safe, and dry.

When he saw that even the Spirit of the Storm could not injure Ko-chin-ni-na-ko, Masts-tru-oi slid down the clouds until he reached the earth. Then he sent his friend away and attacked Spider Woman's house.

Just in time, the two women armed themselves with darts made of flint.

As Masts-tru-oi broke through the door of Spider Woman's house, the two women attacked his legs. They struck so many times that finally he toppled.

Soon afterward, Masts-tru-oi died. Ko-chin-ni-na-ko and Spider Woman carried his remains away from the house and laid them on the plains.

A few days later, Ko-chin-ni-na-ko gave birth to twin sons. She stayed at the home of Spider Woman until it was safe to travel back to the village of her father. By then, all that was left of Masts-tru-oi were bones, bleached pure white by the sun.

For many years, the bones lay there. Ko-chin-ni-na-ko raised her sons in the house of her father and erased the memory of that evil time from her heart. But Masts-tru-oi's friend, the Spirit of the Storm, never got over his grief.

Finally one day the Storm Spirit's mother, the Spirit of Reason, sent a fly out to search for Masts-tru-oi's remains. Then she requested her sister, the Spirit of Memory, to bring the bones of her son's friend back.

The Spirit of Reason arranged the bones, laid a heart among them, and covered them with a cloth. Standing on the north side of the bones, she stretched out her arms and said, "Bones come together. Pa pa pa pa pa."

The bones rattled and assembled themselves beneath the cloth.

Then she stood on the east side of the bones and repeated, with outstretched arms, "Bones come together. Pa pa pa pa pa."

The bones shook some more, then joined one another to form a proper skeleton.

Standing on the south side of the body, the Spirit of Reason said, "Bones come to life."

Flesh formed around the bones. She could hear the heart beat.

Finally, standing on the west side of the body, still with her arms stretched out, the Spirit of Reason said, "Bones, rise up."

Masts-tru-oi stood in front of her. The only difference between the old Masts-tru-oi and the new was that a different heart beat inside him.

The Spirit of Reason told him that his bad deeds had killed him. Then she sent him home to his house on the ledge.

From that day on, Masts-tru-oi was another man. At first, his mother scarcely saw him or heard him, and she would not have believed it possible that he had changed. But gradually his many kind deeds took her blindness and her deafness away. Slowly she felt herself come back to life. Slowly she gained faith in his transformation.

Together, mother and son lived happily for many more years in their home on the side of the cliff.

SPIDER WOMAN

SPIDER WOMAN APPEARS IN NATIVE AMERICAN STORIES FROM Alaska to the southern Great Plains. Her other names include Mrs. Spider, Spider Old Woman, and Grandmother Spider.

Although it might appear to non-Indians that Spider Woman is like the Fairy Godmother of European tales, she is far more complex and powerful than that. In Hopi stories, Spider Woman, or Spider Grandmother, as she is called, is both the messenger of the Sun and the grandmother of the Sun. She is the creator; she rules the earth and is the mother of all life. It was Spider Woman who decided that women would be the ones to build the house, and that the family name would pass through her. And it was Spider Woman who decided that men should build kivas underground and make sand paintings.

In Pueblo tales from New Mexico, Spider Woman creates order from chaos by drawing two intersecting lines with cornmeal, the first from north to south and the second from east to west. This is the beginning of the four directions. It is she who creates the four seasons and adds the four elements of weather—thunder, lightning, clouds, and rainbow—to the sky.

According to traditions of the Keresan people of New Mexico, Spider Woman was once a real human being with supernatural powers. One time, two scouts asked Spider Woman where they could find the door behind which the supernatural beings known as Kachinas lived. Spider Woman said they must promise never to reveal who had told them the secret, and they agreed. Old Badger Woman could open the door, she said.

The scouts found Old Badger Woman and asked her to open the door. "Who told you I could do that?" she asked.

"Spider Old Woman," they replied.

That made Badger Woman furious, and she cursed Spider Woman, turning her and all her descendants into spiders.

It is said today that nonbelievers just see a little spider. But Spider Woman herself still appears to those who know and believe.

ANCIENT CUSTODY BATTLES

 IN OTHER VARIATIONS OF THE STORY OF KO-CHIN-ni-na-ko, she falls in love because the man is so kind to her. It is only when he gets her home that his true nature is revealed: he feeds her bread made from dough mixed with human blood. In that version, although she escapes safely, he remains alive. He kidnaps their sons, and the price she pays for her freedom is that she never sees them again.

CONNECTING THE STORY TO YOUR LIFE

1. Find a quiet, comfortable place to relax and let your mind float. Think back over the various people in the story—the mother, Masts-tru-oi, Ko-chin-ni-na-ko, Spider Woman, the Spirit of the Storm, the Spirit of Memory, the Spirit of Reason. Which ones do you identify with? Why?

What part of this story evoked the most feelings for you? What were those feelings? What incidents in your life are they related to?

Was there any part of the story that made you laugh, or cry, that frightened you or annoyed you or made you angry? If so, go back over these parts. What connections do they have to your life?

2. Close your eyes and go through this story another time. This time, visualize yourself as Ko-chin-ni-na-ko. Relive her excitement at finding such a wonderful husband. Picture her agony and her fright as she discovers the truth, her sense of defeat when he presents her with the first impossible task, her disbelief and excitement when Spider Woman helps her. Picture yourself as Ko-chin-ni-na-ko, dangling in the air, sliding down the cliff, clinging to Spider Woman's web, knowing that if you look back, you will die. Imagine Masts-tru-oi chasing you. Imagine yourself fighting, with Spider Woman's help.

What experiences in your own life correspond to those in Ko-chin-ni-na-ko's life?

What events in your life, in the present or past, correlate to the impossible tasks Ko-chin-ni-na-ko faced? Who was your ally in dealing with past tasks? What allies do you have today?

What men or women in your life have been out of control and

acted like Masts-tru-oi? Have there been times in your own life when you yourself were out of control? Why? Looking back, how do you feel about them now?

End this visualization exercise by picturing yourself as Ko-chin-ni-na-ko, safe now at home with your family and the people you love. Imagine yourself healing and going on with your life.

3. One of Ko-chin-ni-na-ko's gifts to us is the reminder that we can't change the brutal people we are attached to. We can only escape them. If by some miracle they are to be transformed, it will not be by us.

In addition to being a murderer, Masts-tru-oi is a classic crazymaker. He makes impossible demands. No matter what his wife does, he isn't satisfied. He has a frantic need to be in control. He requires other people to revolve their lives around him. He thinks he is the only person on earth that matters. He blames others for all his faults. He creates endless dramas. He does everything he can to keep the people around him off balance emotionally. Behind all his demands lie hidden agendas. When faced with the truth, he gets furious. Like a toddler frozen forever in midtantrum, Masts-tru-oi refuses to grow up.

Who are the crazymakers in your own life? What do they have in common with Masts-tru-oi? How did they get into your life? In what ways do they commit soul murder? (How do they go about destroying you or other people emotionally and/or spiritually?) What steps can you take to reclaim your personal power and get them out of your life?

Visualize yourself telling Spider Woman about the crazymaker. Visualize her instilling you with the courage and strength to remove the crazymaker from your life. Make a painting, a poem, or some other kind of artwork that, in your mind, helps take their power away.

If for some reason you feel you absolutely can't remove the crazymaker from your life, make a list of ten ways you can defuse the crazymaker's power and help yourself feel separate, whole, and more in control of your own life. Write up a six-week plan, a six-month plan, and a one-year plan for enacting these changes.

4. By the time Masts-tru-oi reaches adulthood, he has become obsessed with an impossible goal: finding the perfect woman, someone who can meet his needs. His obsession causes him to brutalize his mother and murder his wives. It also completely prevents his growth and development into anything resembling a well-rounded human being.

Think of the obsessions in your own life, or in the life of someone you know. Where do these obsessions come from? Some childhood trauma? Some adult problem? When do you feel most free of the obsession? Most possessed by it? What difficulties does this obsession create for you?

Sit in a quiet place and visualize your obsession dying, its bones lying bleached in the desert sands. Now picture the Spirit of Reason putting a new heart in the obsession and transforming it into a healthy force, a positive aspect of life.

5. Picture yourself as Masts-tru-oi's mother. Imagine the helplessness she must have felt as she watched her son grow increasingly monstrous. Living with him, watching his evil deeds, caused her to go deaf and blind. She wasn't willing to give her son up. She didn't have the power to make him stop murdering people. So she sank into a state of deep denial, symbolized by the deafness and blindness.

Think of someone you are close to. What areas is this person in denial about? How does his or her denial affect your life?

Denial leaves many clues. Being in denial about something can make you exhausted. It can leave you fuzzy-headed. It can generate enormous anger. It can make you depressed.

Look for clues to denial in your own life.

Who are the people in your life to whom you have handed

over the power of your own destiny, now or in the past? How did you get it back, or how do you plan to get it back?

Close your eyes and visualize yourself as Masts-tru-oi's mother again, this time as an old woman when her son comes back to life. Picture yourself reclaiming your sight, your hearing. Picture your joy at discovering that at last your son is a normal, healthy, whole human being.

6. Visualize the two sisters, the Spirit of Memory and the Spirit of Reason. If you could go to them with a request, as the Spirit of the Storm does, what would it be? Picture these two powerful women as your allies, helping you make decisions, helping you deal with transitions, helping you reach your goals and make your dreams come true. Select four objects that somehow remind you of the Spirit of Reason and the Spirit of Memory and place them on your shrine, one in each of the four directions.

7. Visualize yourself as an ancient storyteller, sitting around a fire. You are the person of honor at this gathering. Listeners sit around the fire in a circle, leaning toward you to catch your every nuance and tone. Tell stories from your own life which have come into your mind as you think about Ko-chin-ni-na-ko, Spider Woman, and the other people and events in this tale.

Chapter Two

Spider Woman's Web

An Athabaskan Tale

Spider Woman rights wrongs. She restores harmony. She returns life to its intended balance. And she cares as much for men who find themselves in danger as for women.

Spider Woman enters and leaves this tale from the Athabaskan peoples of the Far North within just a few paragraphs. But her presence and her actions show the role that feminine energy plays in restoring order and harmony during times of upheaval and chaos.

At the end of the story an ordinary woman living in difficult circumstances is able to reclaim her life.

Once a young man lived contentedly with his two wives, who were sisters. In the summer they lived in a comfortable house made of bark and poles. In the winter they lived in a warm house covered with animal skins. A little distance off lived his parents.

Then the young man's mother died. Her husband, the young man's father, had no sisters, so he came to live with the young man and his wives.

At first, all went well.

The old man saw that his son was vigorous and healthy. He saw that the young man was happy with his wives and treated both of them tenderly and lovingly. The young man made fine snares for trapping grizzly bears, and straight, powerful lances. When the young man constructed a fish weir, it caught more fish than any other weir his father had ever seen.

As time passed, the old man grew jealous.

One day, the young man went out searching for feathers to put on his arrows. Secretly, his father followed. The son reached a tall tree and looked up. High in the upper branches a hawk had built a nest. The young man knew the nest would contain just the feathers he needed, so he took off his fringed shirt and his knee-high moccasins and began to climb the tree.

When the old man saw the young man climbing, he used the magic he had learned over the years and made the tree grow. Higher and higher it rose, until the young man and the top of the tree merged into a tiny speck in the sky. Using his magic once more, the old man stripped all the bark from the tree so that the trunk would be too slippery to descend. Then he returned to the log house and his son's two wives.

The next morning, when the young man had not returned, the old man told the two sisters, "Your husband is dead. We must burn the house and everything in it and go away." The women protested, but the old man told them that he was their husband now.

Silently the women watched as the bark house caught fire and burned to the ground, with all their husband's possessions and tools inside.

One of the sisters was fond of the old man and was willing enough to become his wife. But the other woman loved her husband very much, and she didn't trust the old man. Each time they came to the end of a day's journey, she would take her little boy and go off and make a separate fire for herself, away from the old man, where she heated stones to drop into her bark cooking baskets.

Meanwhile, the young man was trapped high in the tree. Nothing he had learned to depend on could help him now—not his clothes to keep him warm, nor his fishing equipment to supply his food, nor his wives to provide him company, nor his father to remind him of his mother and his youth.

Because he was naked, he grew terribly cold, so he wove feathers into his long black hair and in this way created a blanket to warm himself. He made friends with the birds who lived in the tree, and they brought him food so that he didn't starve.

The man lived this way a long time. He had everything he needed in order to survive, but he missed his wives, his son, and his father. He missed his old life. He wanted to go home. A few times the birds tried to lift him and carry him down to the earth, but he was too heavy for them.

Finally one day, the young man looked out of the branches at the top of the tree and saw a woman coming, far away. She was very old. Her back was bent, and she walked slowly, supporting her weight with two sticks, one in each hand. Even from a distance he could see that she was wearing a long, beautiful shirt. It was decorated with dyed porcupine quills laid in horizontal and vertical bands.

The old woman reached the tree, set down the sticks, and began to climb. The young man watched. It puzzled him that the old woman could climb so quickly and easily. He wondered how she could find a place to grip the barkless wood that prevented him from escaping. Why didn't she remove her beautiful shirt before she began climbing? He worried that she would be stuck up there forever, just like him.

But when the old woman reached the young man, he saw that it was Spider Woman. The shirt was not a shirt, but the markings on her body.

Without speaking, Spider Woman smiled at him. Then she spun an enormous web for him to make a rope with. When he had finished, he thanked Spider Woman and climbed down to the ground.

The man hurried back to his old house, but found only ashes. He searched until he found a faint trail, then set out again.

For many days he followed the trail, until finally he saw his wives and his father far in the distance.

One of his wives was traveling happily with the old man. She had clearly forgotten her young husband. But the other wife trailed far behind with her son, carrying their possessions in a large basket she had woven from strips of bark.

The little boy looked back and shouted, "There's my father!"

"It can't be," the woman replied. "He has been dead now for a very long time."

But as the stranger came closer, the woman saw that it was indeed her husband. She stopped and waited for him to catch up.

He told her about the tree and the treachery of his father and how Spider Woman had saved him. She told him all that had happened since he had disappeared. Then she put her husband into the basket, covered him with a blanket, and carried him back to the old man's camp.

She set the basket down close to the fire, but the old man lifted it and moved it far away.

The woman carried the basket back to the fire.

This time, as she approached the fire, the young man leapt out. First he struck his father, killing him. Then he killed the wife who had betrayed him. Then he and the faithful wife and their little boy returned to the area where they had formerly lived and built another house.

MESSAGES FROM SPIDER WOMAN

EVEN TODAY, TRADITIONALISTS AMONG THE Athabaskan-speaking Navajos of the Southwest consider a spider's web to have special powers. A woman who is working through some difficulty in her life may sit in front of a spiderweb and contemplate its structure. After a while, Spider Woman's messenger, the wind, will bring the answers she is seeking.

Afterward, the woman who has received the messages will sing a song or chant to allow the message to work all the way into her heart.

A Navajo weaver may also seek technical advice from Spider Woman. First the weaver sprinkles corn pollen on a spiderweb. Then she rolls the web into a ball and asks Spider Woman to bless her by giving her designs for her weaving.

THE MURDEROUS MOTHER

 LAKOTA (SIOUX) STORYTELLERS RELATE A TALE SIMilar in theme to "Spider Woman's Web": a mother is jealous of her grown daughter and wants her daughter's husband for herself. The older woman kills her daughter, then disguises herself as the younger woman. But the husband isn't fooled. He finds his wife and restores her to life. Then he arranges for the earth to open up and swallow the murderous mother.

CONNECTING THE STORY TO YOUR LIFE

1. One school of psychology holds that in a dream or a mythic tale all the characters represent different aspects of the same person. The two sisters are different sides of one woman. The father and son are two aspects of one man. Together man and woman represent different dimensions of one person. Even Spider Woman represents a part of this person. She is the transcendent part of us, the creative part of us, the part that can solve unsolvable problems.

From that perspective, this tale is a metaphor for personal growth, and the turmoil that can take place inside us when different parts of ourselves compete for dominance.

Sit quietly in a comfortable place and close your eyes. Go back over the story again, picturing each of these people as different parts of yourself. At what points in your life have you acted in ways reminiscent of each person? At what point in the story is your life at now?

2. Picture yourself as the young man trapped at the top of the tree. Earth is so far below you that you feel completely cut off and isolated. Your father has left you to die. If you don't do something soon, you will freeze or starve to death. What inner strengths can you call on that keep you from simply letting go and crashing to your death?

At what points in your own life has it seemed as if everything you knew about yourself and the people around you suddenly wasn't true, as if all the old methods of dealing with life were suddenly useless? What did you do to survive? In what ways did you have to rely on your own wits and your own inner resources — to create a blanket made of feathers and your own hair, so to speak? In what ways have you had to rely on help from outsiders — like the birds feeding the young man?

3. Picture yourself as the faithful wife, confused, upset, feeling as if life has suddenly gone out of control. Imagine what she is going through emotionally as she watches her husband's father burn the house down. Imagine her internal struggles as she debates what to do, watches her sister change allegiance, and sets boundaries that isolate her from both of them.

At what points in your own life have you had to set boundaries to protect yourself from people who claimed to love you and have your best interests at heart? How did you feel? How did you deal with the emotional isolation? How did you manage to maintain your boundaries?

4. From Alaska to the Southwest, it is common in the traditions of Athabaskan-speaking peoples to burn the house after someone dies. But the fire in this story is more than just an ancient tradition. In a metaphorical sense the fire is like an eraser: with it, the father is attempting to erase that part of life which he doesn't want to deal with. But eventually the very part he tried to eliminate comes back and destroys him.

What parts of yourself have you tried to erase? What parts of you have other people tried to erase? What have you done to reclaim the missing parts of yourself? What work do you still have to do?

5. If the faithful wife, her child, and her husband represent the healthy, whole, growing parts of us, then the father represents our wounded side—the damaged part of us that, in extreme cases, could actually cause our own destruction or the destruction of someone we love. The unfaithful wife represents a naïve, undeveloped, fearful aspect that can cause us to accept other people's view of the world without question and, in extreme cases, cause us to let another person take control of our lives.

The deaths of the parts of the self represented by the treacherous father and the unfaithful wife represent the attainment of a new level of maturity and safety. As we achieve integration and wholeness, there is no longer any danger that some cut-off part of ourselves will betray us.

When do you feel most like the faithful wife or the young man: most vital and alive, most healthy and whole, most able to chart a path through a difficult or impossible situation?

What problems have you had with betrayal in your own life? Who has betrayed you and whom have you betrayed?

Who are you jealous of, and why? If our jealousies are road maps to neglected parts of ourselves, as some psychologists believe, then what are your jealousies telling you? Have you ever been in a situation when normal human jealousies grew so out of control that they led to someone's destruction?

6. Close your eyes and replay the part of the story in which Spider Woman rescues the trapped young man. Notice that although he has survived well in an impossible situation, he is cut off from everything he knows and loves. Spider Woman gives him the means to correct that imbalance, but he himself must use the materials she gives him to make the rope that allows him to escape.

What person, force, or power in your life, either within you or outside of you, functions like Spider Woman?

What, in your own life, would be the equivalent of Spider Woman's Web—something that would help you break out of a difficult situation you feel trapped by? Picture yourself braiding a strong rope from the webbing, then sliding down the tree and heading off to restore balance and harmony to your life.

Some night, just before you fall asleep, or some morning just as you awaken, replay this scene in your head, and see if you can hold on to the images and associations that come into your head.

Use the images that have come to you to create a piece of art—a collage, a painting, a song, a poem—that relates to your own life, to your own role as the starring actor in your own personal tale.

Chapter Three

Qi-yo Ke-pe, the Great Healer

A Tale from the Keresan Pueblos

Some anthropologists believe that the first human societies around the world were open, egalitarian, and well-balanced between men and women. Or they may have been oriented primarily toward women and the power of the feminine. At some unknown point, a patriarchal, male-oriented society replaced the old system. Increasingly, women and the power of the feminine were repressed.

How did this happen, and why? No one knows. This tale from the Keresan-speaking Pueblo peoples of the Southwest offers a metaphorical explanation, and describes the consequences of the loss of the feminine in everyday life.

O nce, long ago, the People lived far, far from here in the village of Kush Kut-ret, on the banks of an enormous river.

The leader of this village had four beautiful daughters. He loved them all dearly and took good care of them.

One day one of his daughters fell ill. Scales and sores covered her body from head to toe.

Her father called in all the medicine men.

They chanted.

They recited incantations.

They painted her with the sacred colors of the four directions.

They consulted with each other, trying to find a cure. But nothing worked.

Night and day the girl's skin itched. The sores burned. Her father suffered terribly to see how miserable she was.

Finally he decided to send for the most powerful medicine person of all, a woman named Qi-yo Ke-pe. She lived far, far to the west in a thatched house made of enormous leaves.

The chief called in the bravest man in the village, the war captain, and sent him off to find the medicine woman and bring her back to Kush Kut-ret.

For weeks the war captain traveled. He crossed a wide river, treacherous and deep, only to reach a second fast-flowing river, then a third and a fourth.

After overcoming these and many other obstacles, the war captain finally reached the home of the medicine woman, Qi-yo Ke-pe. He told her about the sick young woman, and she agreed to return with him to Kush Kut-ret.

When they arrived at the first river, Qi-yo Ke-pe removed one of her moccasins. He thought she was going to empty sand out of it, but instead, when she shook it, herds of deer, antelope, and buffalo leapt out and filled the forests and plains.

None of these animals had existed until then.

The war captain was frightened. He rushed the old woman across the river and hurried her along until they came to the second river.

Again Qi-yo Ke-pe took off a moccasin and shook it, as if to shake out sand. This time, birds flew out, all different sizes, shapes, and colors.

This terrified the war captain even more. Once again he hurried the old woman onward, hoping to avoid disaster before they reached Kush Kut-ret.

At the banks of the third river, the war captain trembled as the woman removed a moccasin again. All kinds of lizards and snakes slithered off, searching for homes among the marshes, plains, hills, and rocks.

When they reached the fourth river, insects of all kinds buzzed forth from Qi-yo Ke-pe's moccasin.

If there had been more rivers to cross, the war captain, known for his great bravery, would have died of fright.

But soon they reached the village of Kush Kut-ret.

The chief's daughter lay terribly ill. She was feverish and did not know where she was or who she was. Blood was caked in her finger-nails from scratching. Pus oozed from the sores on her skin.

To see her, it was impossible to believe that she had ever looked young and beautiful, or that she could ever recover her beauty.

The medicine men stood back and watched. They did not believe this old woman could possibly heal the chief's daughter when they themselves could not.

Quietly, Qi-yo Ke-pe began the healing rituals. She asked for water, and bathed the ill girl.

The medicine men laughed at her. They believed that if their incantations and songs didn't work, ordinary water could not pos-sibly have any effect.

Qi-yo Ke-pe ignored them.

For four days, she repeated this ritual, bathing the girl in water.

By the end of the fourth day the chief's daughter looked as young and beautiful as she had before the disease struck.

The medicine men were furious. "This woman makes us look weak," said one. "She's robbing us of our power," said another. "Peo-ple will no longer believe in us, or send for us when someone gets sick," said a third.

They decided to kill Qi-yo Ke-pe.

The leader of the village was so happy about his daughter's re-covery that he didn't even notice the anger of the medicine men. He thanked the old woman and sent the war captain to guide her home.

The medicine men followed in secret, staying just far enough behind so that the war captain never saw them or suspected they were there. He returned the medicine woman safely to her home.

The medicine men arrived at Qi-yo Ke-pe's home.

"Come in," she said. "You must be very tired. Eat, and rest."

But the medicine men refused. "We have come to kill you," one of them said. "In four days we will return. Then you and your family will die."

After they left, the old woman shaded her eyes with her hand and stared out at the sun. Then she picked up a broom and swept the floor of her home.

As she swept, she sang this song:

> *"Qi-yo Ke-pe is not like you.*
> *Qi-yo Ke-pe would never stoop*
> *to think what you have thought,*
> *or do what you have done.*
>
> *"The years will come and go,*
> *tens and tens and tens and tens,*
> *before the scars will fade,*
> *before the troubles end,*
> *because you murder Qi-yo Ke-pe."*

Four days later, the medicine men returned. They killed Qi-yo Ke-pe, her husband, her son, and her daughter. Then they left.

At the moment when Qi-yo Ke-pe died, all the animals began to mourn. All the birds fell grieving from the sky. All the insects and bees buzzed with sorrow. All the snakes and lizards hid themselves in sadness.

From then on, there was grief. Many times, when people fell ill, there was no one on earth to heal them. Qi-yo Ke-pe was gone. The medicine men had killed her.

SONGS OF HEALING

 IN MANY TRADITIONS, SONGS BY THEIR
nature were believed to hold the power to
heal. Still, certain songs, like the Nightway chant of the Navajos,
include passages dedicated specifically to healing.

Healing is often associated with women or the power of the feminine. In the following song from the Nightway chant, the woman
owns the hogan, the family home.

Round or octagonal, the hogan is built of mud and logs. No
matter where a hogan sits on the landscape, its doorway always faces
the rising sun.

> *Hogan formed from dusk and dawn,*
> *Hogan formed of mist and gloom,*
> *Hogan formed of rain and clouds,*
> *Hogan formed of insects buzzing.*
>
> *A fog of darkness knocks.*
> *Darkness is the path*
> *That leads out of darkness.*
>
> *Let my legs stand again.*
> *Let my feet walk again.*
> *Let my body move again.*
> *Restore my mind to me.*
>
> *Feeling soothed, may I wander.*
> *Feeling cooled, may I wander.*
> *Feeling healed, may I wander.*
> *May I wander free of pain.*
>
> *May there be beauty before me.*
> *May there be beauty behind me.*
> *May there be beauty above me.*

May there be beauty below me.
May there be beauty all around.

In beauty it is finished.

THE WISE OLD WOMAN AND THE MEDICINE MEN

STORIES THAT CONTRAST THE SHORTCOMINGS OF medicine men or holy men with the strengths of a wise and powerful old woman are infrequent but widespread. In a Cheyenne story, a wise old woman lives deep inside a spring. She knows that people are starving, and she wants to help. So she gives the same dream to two medicine men. In the dream she tells each how to dress: in a beautiful buffalo robe, with his face painted just so and his feathers arranged just a certain way.

When the two medicine men discover that they have dressed exactly alike, each accuses the other of making fun of him by imitating his dress.

Meanwhile the people are starving.

When the two men learn of each other's dream, they go to the spring and dare each other to jump in.

Both leap in. At the bottom of the spring, the wise old woman gives each man a bowl of food to take back to the people. It seems like such a small amount of food, but when people begin to eat, the bowls keep filling themselves from within. No matter how much people eat, the bowls never empty. The people are saved.

CONNECTING THE STORY TO YOUR LIFE

1. If you were to cast characters from your own life as players in this drama, who would you be? Who would be the concerned father? Who would be the ill daughter? Who would be the self-centered medicine men? Who would be Qi-yo Ke-pe?

2. Have there been any points in your life when you have acted self-centered and destructive like the medicine men? What caused you to act that way? What techniques did you use to break out of that pattern?

Have there been people in your life like the mindless medicine men? What do you think produced this destructive response in them?

Create a song like Qi-yo Ke-pe's song, about such people in your life. Or create your own healing song like the song from the Navajo Nightway chant. What is the meaning, for you, of the words "Darkness is the path / That leads out of darkness"?

3. Picture yourself as the beautiful young woman, struck by an incurable ailment that robs you of your beauty or your sense of yourself. Picture yourself enduring this ever-advancing destruction. What feelings would you have?

In your own life, what problems, traumas, or crises have robbed you, for a few days or longer, of your own inner beauty or your own sense of yourself? What healed you and restored your sense of centeredness and your sense of yourself?

In the story, the young woman's father wants to heal her for unselfish reasons—he loves her. The medicine men want to heal her for selfish reasons—to prove their own strength and power. But no male power, positive or negative, can heal her. Only the wise old woman, Qi-yo Ke-pe, can restore her.

Have there been points in your life when you found that the only thing that would heal you was some connection with some mother figure, or with the feminine side of the universe? Create a story, a song, a poem, or a painting about this moment or period in your life.

4. In cultures around the world, water is an ancient symbol of healing, cleansing, and the power of the 'feminine. In "Qi-yo Kepe, the Great Healer," the village, an archetypal symbol of human settlement, sits on the banks of a great river. Water rushes past night and day, so water is the most ordinary, common, taken-for-granted aspect of life. But that same water heals the ill woman when all the other rituals and incantations fail.

What does the healing water in the story mean to you? What basic elements of everyday life do you find soothing or healing?

Think of all the different forms of water you have ever encountered in nature, from raindrops to waterfalls, from oceans to mountain springs. What positive associations do you have with water? In what ways do you find water healing?

For the war captain, the bravest man in the village, the four rivers he encounters are obstacles, not delights. Do you have any negative associations with water? What are they?

If you remember your dreams, what role does water play in them? What are your feelings in these dreams?

Take a walk in the rain. Stand underneath a waterfall. Play in the surf. Eat a picnic by a spring. Or plan some other outing in which you can interact with your favorite form of water, whatever it might be.

If you can't do that, find a quiet space where you can be comfortable and undisturbed, and visualize yourself taking such an outing. Feel the water on your skin. Imagine the water healing you, washing away all your troubles and frustrations, all your weaknesses and limitations. Imagine yourself feeling calm, relaxed, whole, at peace.

Create a healing ritual that involves water. What are the elements of your ritual? If possible, perform this ritual, either alone or with friends. If not, find a quiet, comfortable place, close your eyes, and visualize yourself performing that ritual.

Visualize yourself as the young woman, undergoing the healing ministrations of Qi-yo Ke-pe. How do you feel as the dread illness, which no one else could cure, goes away? What is your life like after you have your beauty, health, and vigor back? In what ways are you a different person now than you were before the illness began?

5. Each time Qi-yo Ke-pe reached one of the four rivers, she performed an act of creation. In this sense, the rivers were catalysts to creation, and the moccasins were instruments of creation.

What elements in your life trigger bursts of creativity within you? How could you rearrange your life to increase your creativity levels?

If you could produce four powerful acts of creation, like Qi-yo Ke-pe's, what would those acts be?

6. This story ends with violence and tragedy, not just for Qi-yo Ke-pe, but for all creatures. Why do you think Qi-yo Ke-pe allowed herself and her family to be murdered, without fighting? What are your feelings as you replay this part of the story in your mind? What lessons are there to be learned? What associations come to mind?

Picture yourself as Qi-yo Ke-pe before her death, full of truth, power, dignity, and the ability to create and to heal. What can you do in your own life to restore balance and harmony, to reclaim the power of the feminine, to bring Qi-yo Ke-pe back to life?

Chapter Four

The Woman Whose Heart Became Ice

A Micmac Story

Like the story of Qi-yo Ke-pe, this tale from the Northeast depicts damage to the feminine element of life. As you read, keep a mental or written record of the emotions and associations the narrative brings up for you.

Long, long ago, ten families paddled their canoes up that branch of the river that turns north toward the land of snow and ice. They planned to hunt all winter.

One of the families had a beautiful daughter, just the age to marry. She was pleasant and happy, and very devoted to her parents.

Another family had a son who was looking for a wife. As they paddled upriver toward their winter hunting grounds, the young man watched the girl and fell in love with her.

He asked her to marry him. She refused.

She spoke kindly enough when she said no. But her refusal made him so angry that he vowed to take some terrible revenge on her.

The young man was very knowledgeable in the use of plants. When they reached their winter camp, he went out into the forest, searching for just the right herb, one that can make people unconscious.

One night, he sneaked into the lodge where the young woman and her parents slept. He crushed the herb and held it over the young woman's face, so that she inhaled its essence with each breath. When he was sure she would not awaken, he went out and returned with a snowball. Carefully he set the snowball on the front of her neck, there in the hollow just below her throat.

The young woman was completely unconscious. She did not even stir as the chill of the snowball passed right through her and traveled to her heart.

The next day, she woke up feeling sick and groggy. She shivered with cold. She couldn't bear the thought of eating, and she snapped at her parents for the first time in her life.

This continued for many days. The young woman became thinner and thinner. She didn't look well. She complained, argued, and fought with her parents. Both she and her parents became more and more unhappy.

One day, her mother sent her to the spring to bring back water. But the young woman didn't return.

By now her mother was terribly worried about her. She went out looking for her daughter.

She found her daughter eating snow, stuffing it into her mouth in great handfuls as if she couldn't get enough.

"My daughter, what are you doing?" her mother asked.

"Something burns inside me," the daughter replied. "The only thing that helps is eating snow. Besides, it tastes good. I could eat all the snow in the forest."

Although her mother begged her not to, the young woman stuffed herself with snow every day after that. Each day, she grew angrier, meaner, more difficult to live with. She became so violent and unreasonable that her parents worried she might kill someone.

Finally she said, "My parents, you must kill me. If you don't, I will certainly cause your death."

Her mother was very upset, but she understood that something was terribly wrong with her daughter, and she didn't know what to do.

"You must find seven men, and they must shoot me with seven

arrows each," the girl replied. "If these arrows kill me, all will be well. If not, you will all die."

Her parents understood then that their daughter was no longer a woman. She had become an evil spirit.

The young woman dressed in her most beautiful clothes and sat down in the center of the wigwam.

Meanwhile, her grieving parents asked seven men, all of them famous for their ability to shoot accurately and well, to bring seven arrows each.

Someone suggested that the young woman's parents should tie thongs around her to keep her in place, but she shook her head and sat quietly waiting. For the first time in weeks she felt calm. The only thing she said was, "When I am dead, you must burn me, so that not a single piece of me escapes."

The seven men took their places around the wigwam, and began shooting. They shot one arrow each, all of them squarely into her chest, but she didn't move. Another arrow each, and she still sat alive, smiling at them. A third arrow each, and a fourth. Still she lived. "Keep trying," she encouraged.

A fifth arrow each, and a sixth. Only when the last arrow of the final round struck did she die.

Her parents burned her body. Soon all that remained in the coals was her heart. It would not burn. It was made of solid ice.

For many hours the people continued to feed the fire, until at last the heart of ice melted. Then everyone in the camp packed up and left. Only then did they feel safe.

Her parents grieved for the rest of their days. And from that time on, no one has ever gone near the place where the young woman died. That's because, if even just the tiniest piece of her escaped the fire, and someone were to pick it up, not knowing what it was, that person too would be changed into an evil spirit, determined to kill anyone she met.

A TRAVELING WOMAN

 THE REJECTED SUITOR IS A COMMON theme in Native American stories. Many of these involve murder, revenge, and death. Others are more light-hearted. Some sound contemporary.

Kiowa legends tell of a woman who told a suitor, "I don't want to marry you." When he persisted, she said, "I like to move around a lot. I don't want to stay in one place with you."

The suitor promised to travel with her.

"Let's see how you like it," she suggested.

With him hanging on tightly, she whirled away.

Then he understood that the woman he thought he loved was really a whirlwind. After that, he didn't want anything more to do with her.

SONG TO ATTRACT AFFECTION

 TRYING TO WIN A WOMAN'S AF-fection is another common theme in Native American tales and songs. In this Cherokee song, the narrator asks the powers of the universe to manipulate a woman—without regard for her own well-being—so that she will fall in love with him.

Make the woman sad.
Clothe her in the blue of loneliness,
place her on the earth,
waiting for me.

Make the woman sad.
Let the woman know
that if she comes to me,
she will never be lonely,
she will always be free.
Let her move her soul
into the center of my soul,
so that she will stay forever with me.

Let the woman know
that on the day when clans were born,
the clan she was to join
had one member only,
and that member was me.

Oh, most beautiful of women,
you will wear the white of happiness.
My soul will slide into your soul.
I could never be lonely when I am with you.

CONNECTING THE STORY TO YOUR LIFE

1. What feelings, memories, and associations came up for you when you were reading this story? Write a story or poem, compose a song, or paint a picture that relates to your reaction to this tale.

2. In this story the young man's unchecked—and inappropriate—rage leads to his urge for revenge, and, ultimately, to an innocent young woman's death.

What experiences have you had with the damaging effects of rage, either your own or others'? With the damaging effects of revenge?

The transformation of the young woman from carefree and pleasant to monstrous is a metaphor for the idea that those who have been brutalized often become brutal themselves. So is the idea that someone else could be destroyed just by touching a piece of her.

Looking back on your own life, and the lives of family members and friends, what instances do you find of this principle? What experiences have you had with brutality? How have you avoided becoming brutal yourself?

What techniques have you learned over the years for nurturing yourself when you hurt? For nurturing others when they hurt?

3. If you are a woman, what parts of your own sense of yourself as a woman are most damaged? How did this damage occur? Can you remember what you were like before that? Do you recall times, back then, when you experienced pure joy? What other happy memories do you have from that time? What are you doing to reverse the damage now and to restore the sense of wholeness?

If you are a man, what are your biggest problems in your dealings with women? Do you have these problems with all women—friends, coworkers, family members, etc.? Or do they occur primarily in the context of relationships? Do you have a sense of how these problems developed? What steps are you taking to reduce them?

4. Thinking of your own relationships, have there been times when you felt you were in a situation like this young woman's, or when you have wished you could act like this young man did? What actually happened?

What techniques have you learned over the years for not taking rejections personally? Who are your biggest role models in this area?

What are your patterns in love relationships? How have these patterns changed over the years? How have they remained constant?

Of all the couples you know, which ones in your opinion have the healthiest relationships? Which ones have the most difficult relationships?

5. As in the story of Qi-yo Ke-pe, one lesson here is that evil can destroy any of us, no matter how innocent or undeserving of destruction we are.

How has your own concept of what constitutes evil evolved over the years? Who are the most evil people you know? What makes them evil? How do you counteract their effect on you and your life? Is there some way you could rearrange your life so that you could eliminate them from your world completely?

6. Often in stories like this, when people die from unjust causes, they are resurrected. Cast yourself as the young woman or the young man and retell this story, changing the tale so that it ends on a note of transformation and hope.

Chapter Five

Sedna, Mistress of the Underworld

An Inuit Legend

This tale from the Far North uses betrayal as the theme around which to organize the experiences in the life of a woman named Sedna. Her difficulties with betrayal begin with her own innocence, idealism, and misplaced trust. But even after that, when she is doing her best to take care of herself, she finds herself betrayed in unexpected and brutal ways.

Sedna's story is much more than just a cautionary tale about the dangers of naïveté or the frustrations inherent in relationships. In surviving two profoundly traumatic betrayals, Sedna becomes transformed. She becomes a force of nature. She becomes so powerful that no one can ever betray her again.

In this respect, Sedna's story is a metaphor for the journey from innocence to wisdom, and for the spiritual transition from unthinking vulnerability to something approaching invincibility.

Once, long ago, a man and his wife lived alone, far from other people, on the shores of the great waters. In the summer, they lived in a wooden house and gathered berries and roots. In the winter they lived in a house of ice, and the man hunted seals and caribou, but never polar bears, because only the most courageous hunters could stalk and face the white giant.

While her husband was away hunting, the woman made boots,

mittens, gloves, and other clothing from sealskins and caribou hides. The dogs kept her company.

It was a happy life, and they were content. But then the woman gave birth to a little girl. Soon afterward, the woman died.

After that, the man lived alone on the shores of the ocean with his little daughter, who was named Sedna. Each spring they returned to their summer house, and each fall they built a winter house of snow.

For many years the man and his daughter lived alone, with only each other and the dogs for company. For the man, it was no longer such a happy life, now that his wife was gone. When Sedna was small, he had to do the work of both father and mother, and as she grew older, he had to teach her, as best he could, how to sew clothes and do the other jobs of women. Sometimes he didn't feel like going out in the cold to hunt, or he went out and didn't find anything. Then he and Sedna went hungry.

In spite of the hardships and deprivations, as Sedna grew, she became more and more beautiful. News of her beauty spread across the waterways and tundra. In the winter, young men traveled for many days in dogsleds across the frozen snow, each hoping to convince her to become his wife. In the summer, they arrived in boats made of wood and animal hides.

But Sedna always said no. She didn't believe any of these men had her best interests at heart.

Dozens of young men came and asked her to marry them. But always Sedna answered no.

Through all this her father remained silent.

Finally one winter day a large, beautiful bird flew across the frozen sea and sang a song to Sedna, hoping to win her heart. "Come with me to the land of birds, where no one is ever hungry," he sang. "We will live in a tent made of the most beautiful animal pelts. On the floor, a caribou skin will warm your feet. At night you will sleep on bearskins, soft and warm. During the day you will wear clothes made of the most beautiful feathers. The other birds will bring you anything you wish. The pot that hangs over your fire will always be full of meat. There will always be oil in your lamp."

Sedna listened to the bird's song and admired his colored feathers and thought of the happiness they would have together, living in such comfortable surroundings, with all their needs so easily met.

This time Sedna said yes. She packed up her belongings and called to her dogs.

"You must leave the animals behind," her new husband said.

Sedna started to protest, but then she remembered all the wonderful things he had promised her, and she decided that giving up the animals was a small price to pay. She put on a beautiful coat of sealskins, the last piece of clothing that survived from her mother. She said goodbye to her father and set out alone with her bird husband to cross the frozen wastes.

For days they traveled, then weeks, until she grew almost too exhausted to move. It was so cold that even the sealskin coat failed to keep her warm. Every day her husband said it was only a little farther, but each night they had still not reached his home.

As far as Sedna could see, there was only ice and water. But finally one day, tired and dirty, they arrived in the bird's homeland.

Bird dung covered the snow, caked the tents, and dropped continuously from the sky. Instead of a home made of beautiful animals' skins, she and her husband lived in a miserable tent covered with the thin skins of fish. When the wind blew, the fish skins tore open, and snow piled into the house. Sedna had to watch constantly to keep the snow from extinguishing the fire.

There were no caribou skins on the floor, only ice, and at night, instead of sleeping on a fine bed of bearskins, Sedna lay beside her husband on a cold, hard walrus hide, while the wind blew around them. Instead of having a pot that was always full of meat, she had to subsist on the scraps of fish that the birds brought. Rather than helping her as her husband had promised, the other birds made fun of her. And there was very little privacy.

One day, teasing her, the birds lifted her mother's sealskin coat with their claws. They carried it far out across the water, dropped it, and watched it float away. When Sedna complained to her husband, he told her to stop acting like a spoiled child.

"Oh, how sad I am," Sedna wailed when she was alone. "I should have married one of those young men. I should never have listened to this horrible bird." Every night she lay awake, longing for a way to escape. But there wasn't a single boat in the whole village, and even if she could have managed somehow to work in secret, there wasn't enough wood or animal skins in the entire village to make even a very small boat. And she couldn't leave on foot because she didn't have enough warm clothes or enough strength for such a long journey.

The seasons came and went. Finally one year, after the icy winds of winter gave way to the pleasing breezes of summer, her father left his home and paddled far in his boat, until he reached the new home of his daughter.

He was surprised to find his daughter so unhappy. As he listened to her tales of her husband's treachery, he grew furious. That night, when her bird-husband was sleeping, her father killed him. Then he and Sedna hurried to the boat and paddled hard in the direction of home. Sedna felt relief such as she had never felt before in her life.

When the other birds discovered their dead comrade, they raised a terrible cry of mourning that continues among seabirds to this very day. They also set out to find Sedna and her father.

Soon, in the distance, the birds saw the boat. With their wings, they stirred up the air until they created a huge storm. The waves rose high and threatened to capsize the boat.

Sedna's father didn't want to die. He understood that although he was the one who had killed her husband, it was Sedna the birds were after. To appease them and to save his own life, he threw Sedna overboard.

The astonished woman had just enough strength to grab the edge of the boat before she went down.

When her father saw that Sedna wouldn't let go, he pulled out a knife and cut off the ends of her fingers at the first joint. As they fell into the water, the pieces of finger became whales, and her fingernails became whalebones. With what remained of her fingers, Sedna held on more tightly.

This time, her father cut off her fingers at the second joint. The pieces fell into the water and became seals.

Now the fear-crazed father cut off the remaining stumps of her fingers. But, somehow, Sedna still managed to hang on.

By then, the birds believed Sedna to be dead, and they allowed the storm to fade. No longer afraid, her father let her climb back into the boat.

Sedna was afraid to speak. She looked at the bloody stumps of her fingers, and her whole being turned cold.

When the two travelers arrived at their old summer home, the dogs sniffed Sedna and wagged their tails, happy to see her again. She looked around and wished she could return to the state of innocence she had lived in before.

After her father fell asleep, Sedna lay awake a long time. Finally she rose and called softly to her dogs. At her command, they chewed off her father's hands and feet.

The next morning, when the father woke up and saw what had happened, he cursed loud and long. He cursed himself. He cursed Sedna. He cursed the dogs. He cursed his life.

As the words of the curses died, a great hole opened in the ground. Father, daughter, hut, and dogs all fell in and disappeared. Some say they fell deep into the heart of the earth. Others say they fell all the way to the bottom of the sea.

Either way, they have lived there ever since. And to this very day, Sedna, the motherless woman betrayed by both husband and father, rules as the Mistress of the Underworld. She is the gate to Life and Death. She alone holds the power to heal the body or the soul.

THE TREACHEROUS HUSBAND

LAKOTA (SIOUX) STORYTELLERS TELL OF ANOTHER young woman who for many years refuses all suitors. Finally she marries a handsome, delightful stranger. As they make the long journey to his home, she discovers that beneath the charming exterior is a cruel, violent man. Once they reach his home, she learns that he has married many other young women before her, and eaten them all. He orders his mother to kill this wife, too, but the older woman feels sorry for the young woman and instructs the wife to kill her, instead. The young woman escapes and after many terrifying adventures returns to her home.

"BECAUSE OF YOU AND YOUR WISE THOUGHT"

IN THE LEGENDS OF THE TIWA-SPEAKING PEOPLE OF Taos Pueblo, a young woman travels east and marries. Too late, she discovers that her husband is a cannibal. Although he brings home deer for her to eat, he himself eats human beings every night.

She hates what he is doing and eventually finds a way to kill him. This brings the butchered people back to life. Before they return to their lives, they thank her with these words: "Our daughter, because of you and your wise thought we shall once more enjoy our life in this world."

CONNECTING THE STORY TO YOUR LIFE

On the literal level, this story, like "Spider Woman Saves Ko-chin-ni-na-ko," cautions young women not to choose strangers for husbands. On a deeper level, it shows the dangers when male and female energy become too unbalanced. Especially in the fig-ures of the husband and the father, the story also focuses on the shadow side, which includes those parts of ourselves that we refuse to acknowledge or see clearly. The shadow also symbolizes the potential for evil present in each of us. Like these two men, people who deny their own dark side, or pretend to be anyone other than who they are, run the risk of committing terrible atroc-ities, emotionally or physically.

In concealing the truth about himself and his world from Sedna, the bird husband brutalizes Sedna and ultimately loses his life. To save his own life, the father gives in to the dark wish to sacrifice his daughter—his feminine side. This leads to his death.

At best, denial of the shadow side always results in some kind of betrayal.

1. Divide your life into ten-year intervals (ages one to ten, eleven to twenty, etc.), and make a list of the major betrayals you ex-perienced in each decade.

Who was the main person who betrayed you in each case? What character weakness in that person contributed to the be-trayal? (Was that person in denial? Was that person acting in re-sponse to his or her own unprocessed wounds?)

What, if any, was your role in setting yourself up to be be-trayed?

How did the betrayal change the way you thought, the way you felt, the way you acted?

What parts of yourself did you feel cut off from following the betrayals?

Looking toward the future, can you predict what kinds of betrayals you are potentially still vulnerable to?

Make a list of five characteristics that described you before the pattern of betrayals began and another list of characteristics that describe you now.

2. Create a mythic narrative, similar to the story of Sedna, that describes the betrayal experiences in your own life. Include the missing parts of yourself, represented by Sedna's severed fingers. Include betrayals that you suspect might still come. Conclude with both the positive and the negative transformations that have accompanied the betrayals, or the transformations you still expect to occur.

If you'd prefer, make a collage of items that relate to the betrayals you have survived in your life. Label it "The Story of My Survival" and hang it on the wall where you'll be able to see it every day. This will help you see and accept your past as it actually was. The collage will also become a daily reminder that you have the power to free yourself from the pattern of betrayal.

3. If you are still suffering from the betrayals in your life, create a chant, ritual, or ceremony that will help you heal and help restore harmony to your life.

If you live near mountains, you might hike to the top of a peak and scatter cornmeal in each of the four directions, asking the powers of the universe to heal you. If you live near the ocean, you might go to the beach and watch the waves, picturing each incoming wave as a force of healing, and imagining your bitterness or your wounds washing away with the outgoing tide.

4. If you have betrayed other people, try to picture the betrayal experience from their perspective. Create a mythic narrative about their lives, based on those betrayal experiences.

If you have not already made amends with these people, ask yourself if you are ready to make amends now. If so, write or call each one. If not, ask yourself what steps you still need to take before you are ready to make amends.

5. Create affirmations related to betrayal that give you a feeling of empowerment. Or write the following affirmations on cards and say them each morning when you first wake up and each evening just before you fall asleep:

a. I see myself and other people as we really are, not as I want us to be.

b. I see and accept the pains of the past, without blame or bitterness. I learn all I can from the past and grow powerful as a result.

c. I surround myself with people who are reliable and trustworthy. I am reliable and trustworthy myself.

d. I pay attention to my feelings. I accept them and treasure them as messages from the wise person inside me.

e. I honor the innate powers within me.

f. I am a part of nature. I am a force of nature. The key to my own healing lies within me.

6. In her role as Mistress of the Underworld, Sedna is a metaphor for the powers of the universe. Imagine yourself journeying to see Sedna and speaking with her about your life. What would you talk about? What petitions and requests would you make? What gifts would you bring her? What gifts would you hope to take away?

Chapter Six

The Worm That Devoured Women

A Cherokee Tale

In this ancient tale from the Cherokee Nation, women and women alone are vulnerable to a fatal threat from an unknown source. Society is paralyzed until balance and harmony are restored.

Long, long ago, before the world was as it is today, the People lived in small villages scattered throughout a broad land, so vast that it took the swiftest runner many days to cross. Some people lived in the hills, others in the valleys, but they all lived in the forest, surrounded by trees of all sorts.

Men hunted and brought home food for their families. Women cooked and wove baskets from white oak. People thought of the trees as their friends. Trees provided firewood, shelter, medicines, and food.

It was a happy life. For as long as anyone could remember, people lived that way without trouble.

Then, one by one, all across this vast land, a hunter would come home with a deer to feed his family and find that something, or someone, had killed and eaten his wife.

As long as a man stayed home, his wife was safe. But the minute he left to go hunting, his wife was in danger from some mysterious force or creature that no living person had ever seen.

As more and more men lost their wives to the mysterious woman eater, despair spread across the land faster than a raging fire. Men couldn't bear to leave their homes, worrying what they would find when they returned. Women were terrified to be left alone. People grew hungry. The children and husbands of those who had been devoured mourned without ceasing.

The people called a council and decided that men should take turns hunting, leaving half the men home to guard the women, while half went out to hunt.

After that, it happened less often that a hunter came home and discovered his wife gone. But people still went hungry. Sometimes small children and elderly people grew weak from hunger, fell ill, and died.

Even the wisest people in the forest could not figure out who was killing and eating the women.

Finally one day a hunter standing on the summit of a mountain looked down across the forest and noticed a certain tree at the edge of the village. It was as tall as other trees, and as straight. But there was something about it that made him stop hunting and stand there silently to watch the tree.

He was just about to give up, when the tree bent in half and pushed its way into a hut at the edge of the village.

Suddenly the man understood. The beast that had been killing women was a giant worm, disguised as a tree.

He rushed back to the village, but not before the worm had eaten the woman it had seized.

That night at the council meeting, people discussed what to do.

The next day, everyone dragged wood together to make a huge bonfire. Then, around the fire, they set up rocks in piles shaped like women.

At dusk, they lit the fire. Then the men headed into the forest, as if they were going to hunt.

As the flames leapt, the shadows cast by the rocks took the shape of dancing women.

The greedy worm that had disguised itself as a tree bent down to devour all those women.

By the time the worm was close enough to see that the women were only rocks, it lost its balance and fell into the fire.

All night the fire burned. When morning came, and the fire died, all that remained of the monster was a tiny inchworm, harmless to all.

For a long time after that, people were afraid of trees. But finally they realized that the monster was really dead, and the land was safe again. Once again, men went hunting without worrying that someone would devour their wives while they were gone. And there was never again any reason to fear that a tree was anything other than a tree.

EATING HUMAN FLESH

 ANTHROPOLOGISTS HAVE discovered evidence of cannibalism among ancient peoples in the Southwest. Native American leaders dispute these findings.

No matter which side is right, traditional tales across the continent contain themes of cannibalism. In one version of "The Two Sisters and Their Aunt," (page 151) the Aunt Bear cooks her murdered sister-in-law and feeds her to the dead woman's unsuspecting daughters. In a Cheyenne story from the Great Plains, a husband kills his wife and feeds her flesh to their children. In a story from northern Canada, a woman's parents wrongly accuse her of killing her brother and sister-in-law and eating them.

Other stories, like "The Worm That Devoured Women," attribute human deaths to the erratic behavior of giants or monsters. More than two thousand miles from the Cherokees' original homeland in the Southeast, the Pueblo Indians of New Mexico told of a monster named Seven Heads that devoured young women.

Metaphorically, cannibalism is a vivid symbol for a psychological phenomenon that occurs worldwide: the psychological devouring of one person by another, sometimes called soul murder. This can occur when one person refuses to allow another person to be himself or herself, or when one person insists on merging psychologically with another. It can also happen when a person is unable to maintain a clear sense of being a separate person and having a separate life.

Traditionally, women have been trained to believe they should merge with their spouses. But the results of merging are often as disastrous for the spirit as cannibalism is for the body.

DEATH SONGS

PEOPLE IN MANY TRIBES AROUND THE COUNTRY hoped that before dying they would have time to sing a death song. Sometimes it was a song that had come to them years earlier in a dream; other times the dying person composed it in the last moments before death.

It was also common for relatives and friends to sing songs for the dying, to make it easier for them to pass from this world to the other.

IN THE GREAT DARKNESS

In the great darkness,
My heart stops beating.
The night rattles toward me.
In the great darkness,
My heartbeat stops.

—*Tohono O'odham*

DO NOT BE AFRAID

Sky and sea last forever.
The earth is eternal.
Old people feel sick.
Do not fear death.

—Crow

MY CHILD, YOU ARE A SPIRIT

My child, you are a spirit.
You go from me today.
My child, you are a spirit.
With this song I make you spirit.

—Chippewa

NO ONE HAS FOUND IT

Like strangers groping in the night,
We have hunted for the path
That skirts around to the far side of death.
But no one has found it.
All paths lead to death.
This is hard to face.

The old women and the old men
Who have already greeted death,
The young women and young men
Who have arrived at the site
Where death stands and waits,
They have not found a way
To sneak around death.

> *We are as they were.*
> *All paths lead to death.*
> *This is hard to face.*

—Omaha

CONNECTING THE STORY TO YOUR LIFE

1. What, in your life, devours you? Are there forces, people, or events in your life that seem to be woman devourers? What are they? What can you do to protect yourself from them, or to eliminate them from your life?

2. Note that the villain in this story is completely unexpected. Often trees appear in traditional stories as the Tree of Life, but the tree here is the Tree of Death. Specifically, an evil force—the worm—is masquerading as a force for good: a tree. This theme of something evil disguised as something good is universal, and forms a core part of human experience. Dropping masks and disguises is a key part of movement toward maturity and wisdom.

What experiences have you had with people masquerading as something they weren't? What damage did their behavior produce in your life?

When have you masqueraded as something other than what you were? What fears or other emotions were behind your masquerade? How did you feel about yourself when you were pretending to be someone you weren't?

Imagine a giant fire into which you are throwing all your masks.

3. In this story, as in "The Woman Whose Heart Became Ice" (page 40), fire is a healing catalyst to eliminate an otherwise unconquerable force.

Find a safe, comfortable, quiet place, and picture a sacred fire, burning just to protect you. What, besides your masks, would you throw into the fire?

Now picture yourself moving back two thousand years. It is nighttime in the forest, and you are alone with the fire. What are your thoughts, feelings, wishes, dreams?

Imagine yourself as an ancient shaman. How would you use fire to heal people with imbalances in their lives?

If you have a fireplace, or access to a safe and convenient fire pit, build a ritual bonfire. Write your problems and difficulties on scraps of paper, and throw them, one after another, into the fire.

4. Like water, fire is a basic element of life that occurs frequently in dreams. If you remember your dreams, start watching for dreams that contain fire. What is the role of the fire in the dreams? Does the fire in the dreams rescue you, or cleanse you, by consuming something that you need to rid yourself of?

5. In this story, people limp along with an only partially effective solution until, in an unexpected place, a man finds the solution that solves the problem. If you have problems in your life that seem unsolvable, make a list of them. What are the only partially effective solutions that you've been getting by with?

Take the lists to a brainstorming session with one or more friends. Write down all the ideas that occur to any of you for more adventurous solutions. Let them percolate down through your consciousness for two weeks. Look at the list again. What leaps out at you as a new or unexpected approach that might work? Rearrange your life so that you can try that approach. If the first solution doesn't work, repeat the process until you find something that does.

6. All of us find ourselves in situations that feel as if they were draining life from us. Metaphorically speaking, these too are the

worms in our lives. Make a list of such situations in your own life. Then write up a one-year plan to reduce the frequency and intensity of such situations. Make a five-year plan to eliminate most or all of these situations. Put these in your journal. Or post the plans on the wall, inside a kitchen cupboard door, or somewhere else where you will see them frequently and be reminded of your long-term goal to rid yourself of the worms.

7. Retell this story as an old-fashioned melodrama entitled "The Attentive Man Saves Womankind." Does it bother you that a man is cast as the hero here? If so, what unpleasant associations and memories does this theme trigger for you? Switch from "The Attentive Man" into a new story, this one weaving those associations and memories from your own life into a tragedy, comedy, farce, or whatever else seems most appropriate.

See if you can use these elements from your own life to produce a story so overdone that it triggers laughter rather than feelings of frustration.

Make a list of ten ways in which you still need to heal in dealing with issues related to men and male energy. Make another one-year plan and five-year plan. Put them in your journal, or post them somewhere where you will see them periodically and be reminded of your goal to attain a sense of balance, harmony, and peace between the male and female elements within you and within your life.

Chapter Seven

White Star Woman and Great Star Man

A Pawnee Tale

In this inspirational tale, Great Star Man and White Star Woman stand as symbols for healthy male and female energy. The story shows the balance that develops within a healthy relationship. It shows that a woman can say, "This is what I need," and that her needs can be fulfilled. It shows the great strength of the bond between men and women. It shows that when the powers of men and women combine, all humankind benefits.

Thousands of years before noted Swiss psychiatrist C. G. Jung developed the theory of the existence of both male and female energy within each of us, this Native American tale and others like it spoke to the same theme. The story of Great Star Man and White Star Woman reminds us that in the union of the male and female within us, a new world is born.

In the beginning, the stars formed the Pathway of Departed Spirits, called the Milky Way today. East of the Pathway resided male energy. West of the Pathway resided female energy.

At this time, the earth was not as we know it today, and everything that happened among the stars was a prophecy of what would happen later among human beings.

In the West lived the Evening Star, whose name was White Star Woman. In the East lived the Morning Star, whose name was Great Star Man.

One day Great Star Man looked across the heavens to the Evening Star and saw that she was very beautiful. He longed to be with her. So he picked up his sacred bundle and set out to journey toward White Star Woman.

The Evening Star saw him traveling toward her and waved to him. But before she would let him join her, she wanted to test him and see what kind of character he possessed. Without his knowledge, she placed ten obstacles in his path to make it difficult for him to approach her.

Great Star Man encountered the first obstacle when the earth opened suddenly and a flood of waters swept past. From inside the water, a giant snake rose and spread its jaws wide to devour Great Star Man.

But Great Star Man kept the snake away by singing a sacred song. Then he reached into his sacred bundle and pulled out a ball of fire. As he sang, he threw the ball at the snake, and the monster vanished. The waters disappeared, and the earth closed back up. Once more, Great Star Man's path was level and smooth.

Again and again the obstacles came, and again and again Great Star Man sang his song and used the powers of his sacred bundle to overcome the obstacle. Finally, he approached the lodge of the Evening Star.

But still his ordeal was not finished. Four star beasts guarded White Star Woman: Black Star, Yellow Star, White Star, and Red Star. Together they represented all that would later belong to the earth. They represented the four directions. They signified the four seasons. They stood for thunder, lightning, clouds, and winds. They were the precursors of the trees that would later grow in the forests: cottonwood, elm, willow, and box-elder. They were the forerunners of animals. They also represented the four colors of corn: black, yellow, white, and red.

As the Morning Star approached, the four star beasts were playing the very same hand game that we still play today—singing and guessing, guessing and singing. When they saw the Morning Star, they stopped and rose up to protect the Evening Star. But neither the power of the seasons, nor the strength of the animals, nor the solidity of the trees, nor the elements of the weather, nor the life-giving force of the corn could protect the Evening Star from the allure of the Morning Star.

Soon Great Star Man stood face to face with White Star Woman. He saw that she was even more beautiful than she had seemed at a distance. She saw that he was even more desirable than he had seemed from farther away.

But still the Evening Star would not let the Morning Star touch her. "A child will be born to us," she told him. "So you must bring me a cradle board. It should be made of cottonwood, covered with the spotted skin of a jaguar, laced with otter skin, and protected by a rainbow hoop of willow."

The four star beasts who had formerly protected White Star Woman helped Great Star Man in his search for the right materials.

Finally he returned and presented White Star Woman with the cradle board. But she was still not ready to give herself to him.

"The child will need something soft to lie on," she told him. So again Great Star Man departed. He tracked down a buffalo, killed it, and skinned it. He tanned the hide with buffalo brains. Then he brought the softest part of the hide to White Star Woman to use as a mat for their child to lie on.

Still she would not have him. "You must find water for me to bathe the child in," she said. So again he left and searched, until he found a spring.

All around the water grew grasses that smelled sweet. They perfumed the water and gave it a pleasant taste. Great Star Man saw that in this special garden the flowers were always blooming and the grasses were always green.

The place where he stood was White Star Woman's garden.

Great Star Man scooped up some of the water and carried it back to White Star Woman, and it became rain, the same rain that someday would fall on the people of the earth and bless them.

At last White Star Woman was satisfied. She embraced Great Star Man, and they became man and wife. Now all the powers that the Morning Star possessed belonged to the Evening Star, too, and all the powers that the Evening Star possessed belonged to the Morning Star, too. Each gave power to the other for the sake of human beings, so that they should be well blessed.

The power of the Morning Star resided in a bed of flint. The powers of the Evening Star included the power of storms. When the flint from the Morning Star passed into the storms of the Evening Star, lightning was born, and the potential was created so that later the people of the earth could make knives, axes, and weapons.

When the Evening Star gave herself to the Morning Star, she gave him a pebble as a sign of her love. He dropped the pebble into the great waters, and slowly the earth formed. When the Morning Star saw this, he reached into his sacred bundle and pulled out the ball of fire. He threw it into the sky, and it became the Sun.

When the Evening Star gave birth to a daughter, she bathed the child in the waters that the Morning Star had brought from her garden. She lay the child on the buffalo hide mat. She carried the baby in the cradle board.

When her daughter had reached a certain age, White Star Woman set the girl on a cloud. She handed her daughter some seeds from the garden and said, "When you reach the earth, plant these." Then the Evening Star sent the cloud on its way down to the earth.

The daughter fell from the cloud like rain and landed on the earth. At first, she didn't know where she was. But then she planted the seeds, and from them grew corn.

For a long time, the daughter of the Evening Star and the Morning Star lived alone. But after a while, a young man appeared, the child of the Sun and the Moon. The daughter of the Evening Star gave herself to the son of the Moon, and the two became man and wife. Their descendants peopled the earth with human beings. And to this day, in the evening we look up in the sky and give thanks to our grandmother, White Star Woman. In the morning we look up again and give thanks to our grandfather, Great Star Man.

THE MOTHERS OF ALL HUMANKIND

 IN RECENT YEARS ANTHROPOLOGY AND genetics have come together to trace the origin of all human beings back to one woman and her daughters. Hundreds of years ago, this idea was already common in Native American traditions.

Among the six Tewa-speaking Pueblo Indian tribes, storytellers talk of two mothers who are the first mothers of all the Tewa. Blue Corn Woman lives near the summer and is the Summer Mother. White Corn Woman lives near ice, and is the Winter Mother. To this day, Tewas are divided into Winter People and Summer People in honor of White Corn Woman and Blue Corn Woman.

Mohave storytellers of Arizona relate that once a terrible flood covered the earth. When the people saw the waters rising, they selected a beautiful young woman and sealed her in a boat that was like a trough with a lid on it. Everyone else died, and only the woman survived.

When the waters receded, the young woman opened the boat and stepped out on dry land. All alone in the world, she lay in the sun to warm up. She became pregnant and had a daughter. Then her daughter became pregnant and bore a son. From these two women, all human beings descend.

THE FOUR DIRECTIONS

 ALTHOUGH DETAILS VARY, tribes across the country honor the four directions. In the story of White Star Woman and Great Star Man, the four directions guard White Star Woman. They're also linked to the seasons, corn, the forces of the weather, and other parts of nature.

Storytellers among the Tewa-speaking Pueblo peoples of New Mexico report that soon after Blue Corn Woman and White Corn Woman sent the first people forth, the four directions were assigned colors. Blue became the color of the North. Yellow was the color of the West. Red was the color of the South, and White the color of the East.

Other tribes assign the four directions other colors.

✋ CONNECTING THE STORY TO YOUR LIFE

Great Star Man embodies the person on a quest. Far away, on the other side of the universe, he sees something he desires, and he sets out to obtain it. Along the way, he must overcome obstacles and battle beasts. When he arrives at his destination, more tasks await him. He performs these and is rewarded by achieving his goal: union with White Star Woman.

White Star Woman embodies the person who knows what her needs are and meets them. In order to avoid the pitfalls of blind trust, she does reality checks again and again: these are the obstacles and tasks that face Great Star Man. Her caution and wisdom result in her becoming the grandmother of all humanity. Without her, human beings would not exist.

1. Find a place where you can be comfortable and quiet. Follow your breathing for a while. Then, if you are a man, visualize yourself first as Great Star Man. If you are a woman, visualize yourself first as White Star Woman. Move through the story, seeing yourself as your character. After you have completed that visualization, picture yourself as the character of the opposite gender, and walk through the story in your mind again, imagining yourself as that person.

When you are finished, write down any insights you may have had about yourself and about your own male and female attributes during the visualizations.

2. In this exercise, you will use the elements of your own life to create a mythic narrative similar to Great Star Man's quest.

Begin by asking yourself what you want in life that seems as far away as the other side of the Milky Way.

Picture yourself preparing a sacred bundle before you start on your quest. What objects would you carry in the bundle to help you in times of trouble? Use concrete, visual symbols to convey abstract meanings. (If you want to carry truth in your sacred bundle, think of some concrete object that to you represents personal truth, such as your private journal.)

Picture obstacles. If they are abstract, such as lack of money or lack of time, turn them into concrete, visual images. For lack of money, you might visualize an empty wallet or a check stamped "insufficient funds"; for lack of time, perhaps a clock with hands that whirl round and round, or a scene in which you are working frantically.

Picture yourself overcoming those obstacles one by one, with the aid of the objects in your sacred bundle. Picture yourself getting safely past the four beasts that surround your goal. Visualize yourself reaching your goal, only to discover that you must finish more tasks before you obtain what you want. Again, turn everything into concrete, visual images.

Picture yourself performing these final tasks and achieving your goal.

3. In this exercise you will again use the elements of your own life to create a mythic narrative, this time based on White Star Woman and her ability to know and meet her needs.

Picture your life. What do you consider your core needs to be? If these are abstract (love, happiness, etc.), find a concrete visual image that represents that abstraction.

Now picture yourself creating tests to determine if some particular solution will truly meet your needs. Again, use concrete visual images to represent abstractions. Think of the four beasts that guard White Star Woman. Imagine four powerful forces of nature guarding you. What would they be? Create concrete visual images to represent these four forces.

Think of the final tasks White Star Woman gives to Great Star Man. What tasks, literal or metaphorical, would you give to a person who wanted to win your love?

Picture yourself as White Star Woman planting a healing garden. What would you plant in the garden? What does each part of the garden symbolize to you?

Picture yourself giving birth to your full powers as a human being. Again, use concrete images to symbolize the abstract.

4. Create your own affirmations related to Great Star Man and White Star Woman. Or use the following, saying them each morning when you first wake up and each night before you fall asleep.

    a. I am Great Star Man. I can travel across the universe and find what I most want.

    b. I am White Star Woman. I know what my needs are, and I meet them.

    c. I am both the grandmother and the grandfather of an entire universe. I embrace the male and female within me. I give birth to my whole self.

d. I am the grandchild of Morning Star and Evening Star. I contain the seeds of everything I want and need within myself.

5. Write a poem about yourself that begins, "I am Great Star Man." Write another that begins, "I am White Star Woman." Concentrate not on rhythms or rhyme, but on speaking your own truth.

6. Paint or draw a picture, even a very simple one, of the two parts of yourself, Great Star Man and White Star Woman, connected by the Milky Way. Personalize this picture with symbols from your own life.

On your shrine make a display that represents the parts of you that are Great Star Man and Great Star Woman.

7. Make a medicine bundle of objects that represent healing forces in your life. Set this bundle in a place of honor, where you will see it every day.

Chapter Eight

Ataensie, the Woman Who Fell from the Sky

An Iroquois Tale

The story of the woman who fell from the sky is one of the core tales from the Northeast. There are as many versions as there are tellers. In some, the man in the beginning is Ataensie's husband, a malevolent person who pushes her off the edge of the sky. In others, she falls, rather than jumps.

Thematically, this story is linked to the final portion of the story of White Star Woman and Great Star Man, where, under much different circumstances, a woman descends from the sky. And the duties outlined for Ataensie at the end of this story are similar to those of Sedna (chapter 5). It could also be said that Ataensie combines the roles of Spider Woman, the Spirit of Reason, and the Spirit of Memory (chapter 1).

On a more personal level, Ataensie's story speaks to us at all ages in our lives. When she was young, she was already strong, determined, clear about who she was and what she needed to do. As an old woman, she remained powerful, but in different ways.

Ataensie is a reminder of our core creativity. She inspires us to use the soggy, unshaped mud of our lives to create our own fully formed, well-balanced worlds.

Eons ago, before human beings existed as we know them today, even before the birth of the earth, supernatural beings lived in the sky. One of them was named Ataensie. She was a beautiful woman, kind, wise, and a powerful healer.

Once, Ataensie was performing healing rituals for a sick man, who lived at one side of the heavens near a beautiful tree. But no matter what chants she sang, nothing worked.

The sick man opened his eyes and whispered, "Last night I dreamed that if I am ever to be healed, that tree over there must be cut down."

For four more days, Ataensie continued to perform the healing rituals of the spirit ancestors. But still the man lay ill, near death. So Ataensie took her stone ax from its leather pouch and began chopping the tree.

The tree was very large, and its trunk was as thick as an elk is tall. But Ataensie was strong. She was patient. She was determined. Blow after blow, she chopped at the tree, until the sun had moved all across the sky from the east to the west.

Just before sunset, the tree fell down. It was so large, tall, and heavy that as it fell, it broke right through the sky, creating an enormous hole.

Ataensie stood at the edge and looked down. Far, far below, so far that if she had had ordinary human eyes, she would have seen nothing at all, she saw the dark primeval waters moving back and forth.

Ataensie went to check on the sick man. He had fallen into the deep sleep of one who is finally healing from terrible wounds. He no longer needed her. She walked to the edge of the hole in the sky and leapt out into space.

Ataensie fell and fell and fell and fell. It seemed as if her fall lasted for whole seasons, for entire years. Finally, she hit the dark waters.

At first she just swam around. But eventually she grew exhausted. A sea turtle appeared. She climbed on his back and rested.

As far as she could see, there was nothing but water.

For a long time, Ataensie floated on the back of the turtle.

Various animals that live in water came to inspect this marvelous being who had appeared in their midst from the sky: a frog, a beaver, a water snake, fish.

One of them brought her a little mud.

Ataensie held it in her hand and said a prayer. Dry land formed, and the earth was born.

Time passed.

When Ataensie saw that the earth was working as it should, she gave birth to a daughter.

Her daughter grew, and, like her mother before her, she became pregnant without lying with a man, because at that time no men existed on earth.

Ataensie's daughter gave birth to twin boys. The first, Ioskeha, was born normally and was a healthy and vigorous baby.

But even before birth, the other twin was evil. He refused to be born by the normal route. Instead, he burst out of his mother through her armpit, causing her to die.

Ataensie buried her daughter, and where her daughter's body lay, the first foods grew. From her breast grew corn. From her arms and legs, beans. From her belly came squash.

Ataensie raised her grandsons. The first was a happy boy, who learned the wisdom of his grandmother. When he grew up, he went about creating lakes and springs because the earth at that time was too dry. Then he opened a cave in the earth, and all the animals that we know today came forth and inhabited the woods and prairies.

But from the moment of his birth, the second twin brought trouble. He fought with his brother. He laughed at Ataensie. He dried up the lakes his brother had created. He chased the animals away, so that people grew hungry.

Eventually, his grandmother banished him from the earth, and he became the ruler of the spirits of the dead.

To this day Ioskeha lives in a cabin off in the East, just at the place where the sun rises. His grandmother, Ataensie the Wise, lives with him. While Ioskeha tends to the running of the world, Ataensie, our grandmother, decides what will happen in our lives. It is she who determines the moment of our birth, she who knows what we need in our lives, and she who decides when we will die. It is she who decides when nations will be born, how they will blossom, and when they will die.

WOMAN AND CREATION

 IN CREATION stories from many tribes, women, female animals, or female forces play a significant role in the formation of the earth. In traditions of the Flathead in the Plateau region, the creator is a woman. Among the Keresan-speaking Pueblo Indians, the creators are Ts'its'tsi'nako, Thought Woman, and her sisters, Naotsete and Uretsete, whom Thought Woman sings into existence. In an alternate manifestation, Thought Woman is Iyatiku, Our Mother, the mother of all humankind. In yet another manifestation, she is Spider Woman herself.

In Hopi tradition Huruing Wuhti, Hard Beings Woman, creates the world. In ancient Cherokee tradition, the creator was the Woman in the River Foam.

THE WOMAN WHO KILLED THE CREATOR

 A FEW NATIVE AMERICAN CREATION STORIES CONtain negative images related to women and women's power. The Quechan people, who live along the Colorado River of southern Arizona and California, say that a powerful spirit-woman named Hanyi caused the death of Kokomaht, the Creator.

CONNECTING THE STORY TO YOUR LIFE

1. Ataensie is an archetype, embodying the powerful woman at all ages in our lives. Make a display on your shrine that honors powerful women you admire, either women you know personally or those you have read about or heard about. Place photographs, books, or other symbols of these women on the shrine. Include some important object from your own life, something that says to you, "This is me."

What traits do you most admire in these women? What traits do you most admire in yourself? What are five ways you could rearrange your life to increase your sense of your own personal power? Draw up plans for rearranging your life in one or more of these ways. What needs to be done in the next thirty days? The next six months? The next two years? Post the plans prominently where you will see them every day, or keep them in your journal.

2. Ataensie's leap from the edge of the sky is an act of faith that leads to creation. What stories do you have from your own life, or the lives of people you know, about times when a leap of faith has produced creative results? Have there been times when the opposite occurred—when you leapt not into creativity but into disaster? What differences can you see between these two kinds of experiences?

What leaps of faith or acts of creation have you been avoiding in your own life? Select the one that is most important to you, or the one that feels safest to you, and take that leap.

3. Ataensie's leap is also an act of intuition. She senses she will be all right, and she trusts that intuition. What role has intuition played in your life?

For the next week, practice catching the fleeting intuitions that flit in and out of your head. Keep a list of them. What pattern do you see? Do you trust your intuitions? Why or why not?

4. The tree is the Tree of Life, but in this story it also represents the status quo, the tried and safe ways of doing things, the old order of life. Unless this old order is uprooted, male energy will die, and female energy will not be free to begin the great task of creation.

Notice that Ataensie doesn't chop the tree down immediately. She gives the old ways one last chance to work before she tries something new.

What does the tree represent in your life? Who is the ill man? In what ways are you like Ataensie? What reality checks do you need to do before you are ready to try something new? What else do you still need to do in order to gain the courage to chop down the tree and get on with the core tasks of your life?

What wounds do the men in your life suffer from? What role do you play in their healing? How does this affect your life, your creativity?

5. Twins are common in stories around the country. Here the two young men stand for duality, for good and evil. They represent two different aspects of male energy. They also stand for the divided self.

Create a narrative about your own life in which you play both roles, the good twin and the difficult twin. Create a song about these two contrasting sides of someone you know well.

Notice that unlike Masts-tru-oi's mother (chapter 1), Ataensie does not simply resign herself to the flaws of her difficult progeny. She also does not punish him for destroying her daughter, his mother, or for his other destructive acts. Instead, she finds a role and a task suitable to his particular talents.

Have you found appropriate roles for those qualities of yourself that are part of the difficult twin?

What work do you still need to do to integrate the conflicting parts of yourself?

6. If you were an ancient storyteller, which version of this story would you tell? The one in which Ataensie jumps from the sky of her own free will? The one in which an evil husband pushes her? Or the one in which she falls? What experiences in your life are related to your choice?

7. As Ataensie swims in the dark waters, she reaches a state of exhaustion. At that moment, a turtle rescues her. At what points in your life have you arrived at a state of complete exhaustion? What played the role of the turtle for you?

Chapter Nine

The Origin of Corn

An Abenaki Tale

This gentle tale from the Northeast shows the life-giving force within women. It shows that when a woman sets her own boundaries and maintains them, she unleashes a great positive force of nature. It also shows that transformations within a woman are both inevitable and startling, and that when a woman allows herself to be transformed, she benefits both the people she is connected to and all humankind.

A very long time ago, soon after people were first created, a man moved far away from any other people. He had no fire, because he did not know about fire. He had no corn, because corn had not yet come into the world. All he had to eat were the natural foods in the forest: roots, bark, ground nuts, berries, and animal flesh.

At first the man was happy because he had plenty of food and a sturdy winter home and fine summer camps. But as time passed, the man began to feel sad because he was alone. He had no companion with whom to gather blueberries. He had no neighbors to whom to give the first kill of the season, no one to play handball with. There was no woman in his lodge to weave strips of basswood bark into carrying bags. There were no children to delight in the sweetness of the sap that flowed from the maple tree.

The man no longer felt like digging roots. He no longer felt like picking nuts, or hunting. The syrup of the maple no longer tasted good to him. He didn't want to eat anything at all.

Instead, he lay down in the sun and fell asleep.

For a long time he lay there, dreaming.

Then one day in his sleep, he sensed a presence close by. He woke up badly frightened.

When he opened his eyes, he saw a woman. She was unlike any other woman he had ever seen. She had long silky hair that was golden and fair.

When the woman spoke, her voice soothed him, and he stopped being frightened.

Just looking at the woman, the man fell in love with her. He wanted to hunt moose and bring the meat and hide home to her. He wanted to shoot pigeons and smell the meat as she roasted the birds. He wanted to sit with her by the fire in winter, and lie with her at night.

He asked the woman to come closer, but she refused. The man tried to approach the woman, but she pulled even farther away.

Not wanting to frighten the woman off, he sat on the ground and sang her a song. He sang about his loneliness; he promised to trap beavers for her, and otters. He begged her not to leave him.

Finally the woman said that if he would do exactly what she told him to do, she would stay with him always.

The man promised to obey.

The woman took his hand and led him to a meadow where the grass was very dry. There she found two dry sticks and told him to rub them together quickly, holding them over the grass.

The man did, and it set the grass on fire. The grass was so dry that the fire spread quickly, flying across the land as fast as an arrow, until the ground lay blackened and bare.

"When the sun goes down, you must take me by the hair and pull me across the ground," the woman told him.

The man didn't want to, but she reminded him that he had promised to do exactly what she said. "If you don't, I will leave," she said.

He wanted her to stay more than anything else on earth, so that night he twisted her long, silken hair around his fist and dragged her across the charred meadow.

When he reached the other side, the woman disappeared. Seeing this, the man collapsed. He felt angry and betrayed. He felt even more lonely than he had before. In sorrow he fell into a deep sleep.

When he awoke, he saw that everywhere the woman's body had touched, a green plant sprouted from the earth. The days passed, and the plants grew tall and developed ears of corn. The golden tassles of the woman's hair topped each one.

It was then that the man understood that the woman had done as she had promised. She had not left him at all. She had only changed form. And to this very day, when people see the yellow silk of her hair on the ears of corn, they understand that Corn Woman has not forgotten them.

SONG OF THE CORN MOTHER

 SONGS AND STORIES FROM ACROSS THE country celebrate corn and the origin of corn. On the Great Plains the Pawnee sing this traditional song:

> *Here comes the Corn Mother.*
> *Say hello to the Corn Mother.*
> *Give thanks to the Corn Mother.*
> *Now she comes.*
> *Here comes the Corn Mother.*

SHE GAVE HER LIFE SO THAT ALL MIGHT LIVE

IN A VARIATION OF "THE ORIGIN OF CORN," ABENaki storytellers recount the story of the First Mother. A great famine came on the people. Finally the First Mother told her husband that the only way to save humankind was to kill her. At first he refused, but she insisted. Where she was buried, the first corn grew, and people were saved from starvation.

CONNECTING THE STORY TO YOUR LIFE

1. Find a comfortable place where you can sit quietly for thirty minutes or more. Close your eyes and go over some of the instances from our reading so far in which women or feminine power was a source of creation, corn, salvation, transformation, etc.

Spider Woman. The Spirit of Memory. The Spirit of Reason. Thought Woman. Our Mother. Qi-yo Ke-pe. The wise old woman in the spring. The woman who resurrected the victims of cannibalism. White Star Woman and her daughter. Ataensie. The woman who gave corn to the earth. . . .

As these names and stories pass in front of you, let your mind float. What positive feelings, memories, and images come to you? Write them down. Make a painting, a song, or a poem, using these images.

If any negative feelings or associations came up for you, write these down, one each, on small pieces of paper. Separate the scraps of paper into two piles: those feelings and associations you are ready to put behind you, and those you feel you still need to work on or work through. Copy the ones from the second pile into a list, and write up a plan for working on or working through these issues. Divide the plan into periods: What can you do in the next month? What can you do in the next year? What can you do in the next five years? Post these somewhere prominently, or keep them with your journal.

Put back together the two piles of negative associations and burn them. Imagine that you are burning the field, preparing for the birth of a new, transformed you.

2. Divide your life into ten-year periods. What major transformations have you undergone during each decade? Include both those that are common to all women, such as puberty, and those that are unique to you. Now think of all your wildest hopes, fantasies, and dreams—anything that would require some major transformation in you or your life. Assume for a moment that you can achieve any of these, if you wish. Choose the three that mean the most to you. Picture yourself achieving them in the coming decade. What changes would you have to make in your life to achieve these dreams?

If you consider any of these dreams impossible, ask yourself why. Make a commitment to read and work through one of the fine manuals available on achieving your dreams—Julia Cameron's *Artist's Way,* for instance. Tape a list of your three most meaningful dreams at the end of the last chapter of that book, or another you choose, and begin reading.

When you finish that last chapter, look at the list again. Do your dreams seem more realistic, more achievable now? Take steps to make at least one of these three dreams come true.

3. Go back over this story again, this time concentrating on the lonely man.

Think of the times in your own life when you have been loneliest. How did these periods resolve themselves? If you are going through a period of loneliness now, take time to sit quietly with your loneliness. Can you make loneliness your friend? What do you find most difficult about loneliness? What do you find easiest? When did this loneliness begin? When and how do you expect it to end?

Create a poem, a prayer, a song, or a series of affirmations about your loneliness.

4. The man in the story wants a human companion. Just when he thinks his dream has been fulfilled, everything changes. Instead of a woman, he gets corn. At first he is upset, until he realizes what a great gift the woman has given him.

Think back over the times in your own life when you thought you were getting what you wanted, only to discover that you got something else instead. Looking back, was what happened actually a gift? If so, create a narrative of the experience, patterned after "The Origin of Corn."

If you feel frustration rather than contentment, write a healing chant for yourself. For the next three weeks, sing or say it to yourself every morning on first awakening and every night just before falling asleep. At the end of that time, give yourself some beautiful gift to complete the healing process. This need not be expensive, but it should be something that has some deep meaning to you: some symbolic equivalent of the corn, something that relates to some hope, dream, transformation, or deep need.

5. In most Native American traditions, corn is not merely a practical part of everyday life. It is a symbol of life itself, of all that is holy and sacred and good.

Buy one or more cobs of multicolored corn and make a decoration with them that you can display somewhere prominently in your home—as a centerpiece for the table, a wall hanging, an item on your personal shrine. For the next week, each time you notice the corn, stop and let your mind float for a moment. What images come to mind?

Make a song, chant, or prayer of thanksgiving for all that is holy, sacred, and good in your own life. If you are ready to change the display on your shrine, lay out objects that stand for these aspects of your life. Include a cob of colored corn, or the display you have made. Use it as a reminder of the links between us and all the men and women who have gone before us on this continent for thousands of years.

Chapter Ten

First Woman and the People

A Navajo Tale

Where stories like the one about Ataensie talk of falling to the present world from the sky, others speak of flying up to the sky in order to reach a new world. In this Navajo story, First Woman helps people pass from one world to another. She helps them learn how to conduct themselves and how to live well. After they let Coyote lead them astray, she puts them back in touch with their basic values.

L ong ago, before human beings had become differentiated from animals, birds, and insects, they all inhabited the Third World. The Third World was much better than the first two worlds had been. The First World was dark and crowded, and fire nearly destroyed all living creatures. In the Second World, famine and wars decimated them.

The Third World was roomy and airy. Mountains marked each of the four directions. There were rivers and springs. Everyone had plenty to eat.

Gradually, humans became distinguishable from animals, most of the time, and birds distinct from insects. Even so, one way or another, all inhabitants of the Third World could still fly.

As generations came and went, and the population grew, the day came when there was no longer enough food. Neighbors fought over tiny scraps, and everyone stole from each other. They planted corn and beans, but they didn't understand the proper methods of planting and harvesting. They didn't know the proper prayers and blessings to ensure good crops. Harvest after harvest failed, and people had to wander far to find a little food. Everyone suffered.

The Four Judges who ruled the Third World sent out messengers to gather all the clans. After much discussion, everyone agreed they must leave the Third World and find a better place. So they all flew into the air and began searching for the hole in the sky through which they could pass into a better land. But although they flew far and wide, they could find no holes or cracks anywhere in the ceiling of the sky.

They were just about to give up when a voice called from the East, "Come over here." In the East, at the edge of the sky, a face covered by a mask looked down on them.

Another voice called from the South. "Come over here. This is the way to reach the world that is above."

From the West came a third voice, and from the North a fourth.

The voices and the masked faces belonged to First Woman, First Girl, First Man, and First Boy. But the inhabitants of the Third World didn't know that.

It was now that the inhabitants of the Third World divided permanently into groups. Those that were to become the First Dine'é— the First People, the first Navajos—listened to the voice of First Woman, calling from the East, and followed her into the Fourth World. There they found a land with mountains and rivers, prairies and hills.

Ever since that day, First Woman has protected the Dine'é.

Meanwhile, the Bird People followed First Girl, who was calling from the South. She led them from there up into the Fourth World, and that is why, even today, birds fly south in the winter.

The voice from the West belonged to First Man. The Animal People followed him into the Fourth World, at a place where there were high mountains on every side. They live in the mountains to this day.

The voice from the North belonged to First Boy. Insects and crawling creatures followed him up into the Fourth World. But it was so cold that they had to crawl into burrows and stay close to each other to keep warm. That is why they still disappear into the earth in the winter.

When the Dine'é arrived in the Fourth World, First Woman had already been living there for some time. She felt embarrassed to see her people looking so ragged.

"Where have you been for so long?" she asked. "Your skin is covered with dirt and filth. You stink as if you'd never bathed. Have you been living like animals in nests and caves?"

She instructed them to wash their bodies and their hair and to fast before she saw them again the next day.

By then the Dine'é had discovered that other people lived in the Fourth World already. Some, like the Hopis, cut their hair in bangs, just above their eyebrows. Others, like the Utes and Comanches, wore their hair in long braids that hung over their shoulders and were decorated with porcupine quills and feathers. Others wore their hair shoulder length. Still others went around with shaved heads, except for one long hank of hair at the very top.

Soon the Dine'é themselves felt embarrassed. For as long as anyone knew, men and women among them had combed their long hair back from the forehead and tied it in the back. But no one in the Fourth World wore their hair that way. Also, many Dine'é still wore animal hides and feather capes, which made them look odd in this new world.

Once they had cleaned themselves, First Woman showed them how to roll their hair into double loops tied back behind their heads. She taught them how to use moccasins, leggings, and other clothing.

Then she pointed to the corn that grew near the stone houses of the Pueblo peoples who already inhabited the Fourth World, and she said, "If you want to stay in this world, you must learn to grow corn." She advised them to settle down near the Pueblo peoples and learn from them. "Work for them, and you can earn your food and enough extra to plant your own fields."

After First Woman left, people began arguing about what to do. Some said there was no need to bother with corn because there were plenty of wild roots, berries, and seeds free for the taking, all around. Others thought they should follow First Woman's advice. Others pointed out that nothing seemed to have changed since they left the Third World. They were still arguing about food, just as they had before.

Coyote was listening. After a while, he stepped into the middle of their circle and said, "There's no reason to work for your food. The Pueblo peoples leave their fields unguarded. You can take all you want."

"The Dine'é do not steal," the People told him.

"Oh, no, it's not stealing," Coyote said. "And anyway, every stalk has a dozen ears of corn. If you just take the bottom ear from each stalk, they'll never even miss it."

That did sound like a much simpler way to get what they needed.

Volunteers offered to go to each of the four directions and gather enough corn to plant crops. Spider Woman herself wove bags for the four corn gatherers to carry.

When the first volunteer returned, he poured out his sack. True to the plan, he had taken only the lowest ear of corn on each stalk, but those ears grew so low, they lay in the water of the irrigation channels. The kernels were useless as seeds.

When the second volunteer returned, he carried only half a sack. Mice had gnawed what corn he had so badly that there was no hope of using it for seed.

The third volunteer had found it easiest to pick only the ears at the very tops of the stalk. Although his sack was full, the cobs were tiny, and worms had devoured most of the kernels. His corn certainly wouldn't do for seed.

When the last volunteer returned, his corn was covered with corn smut and mold.

People realized they should have followed First Woman's advice. But it was too late simply to go live with the Pueblo peoples. Even though the corn the volunteers had brought might be useless, they had to face the unpleasant truth: every ear of it was stolen.

The People called a council and invited First Woman to attend.

"Send four young women out," she advised. "One for each of the four directions, with gifts to exchange for seed corn. Let their brothers accompany them, so they can learn how to plant and how to say blessings and prayers to make the corn grow."

Again Coyote stepped forward and tried to convince the people that what First Woman suggested was too much trouble. But this time, they ran Coyote off and did as First Woman advised. People stationed lookouts on the mesa to watch for the return of the young people. Then they prepared their fields in the broad valley below.

After four months, the first young woman returned from the East, carrying a basket of white corn. Her brother had learned the rituals of the Seed-Blessing Ceremony and the prayers and chants for plantings.

From the South the second young woman returned, carrying a basket of blue corn. Her brother had learned the Corn-Blessing songs.

From the West, the young woman brought yellow corn. Her brother had learned the Growing Ceremony.

From the North, the young woman brought corn that was all different colors. Her brother had learned the Harvest Rites.

Along with the corn, the young people brought beans, squash, pumpkins, tobacco, and other herbs. They brought rain-rattles and medicine bundles. They brought feathered dance headdresses and other ceremonial clothing.

Soon the fields of the Dine'é stretched far toward the horizon, and the harvest was so great that no one went hungry.

From then on, in honor of the four young women who went out

in search of seed, it was women who stored the seeds during the winter, and women who planted the seeds in the spring, after the men had prepared the fields. People knew now never to trust Coyote. They knew the importance of listening to the wise words of First Woman, who helped them again, after that, when they had to move, all at once, from the Fourth World to the Fifth.

THE ORIGIN OF LOVEMAKING

 IN NAVAJO TALES IT IS FIRST WOMAN, ALTSÉ Asdzáá, who creates the genitals of both men and women. She makes the penis from a piece of turquoise. She fashions the vagina from a white shell and the clitoris from a red shell. She teaches the male and female organs how to lie together, and how to please each other.

FIRST WOMAN AND FIRST MAN QUARREL

 NAVAJO STORYTELLERS REPORT THAT FIRST Woman and First Man had a horrendous fight. Some say the fight began when First Man caught First Woman with another lover. Some say it began when First Man's mother-in-law scolded him for thinking he was the center of the universe.

Many people say it began when First Man came home from the hunt. Instead of thanking First Man for the food, First Woman informed him he wasn't really the one doing the hunting. The real hunter, she said, was *shijóózh*, "my vagina." In fact, her vagina did all his work, because if he didn't want sex with her, he wouldn't bother to hunt or do anything else.

First Man stormed away in a rage and moved across the river. All the men went with him. All the women stayed with First Woman.

In the beginning, both men and women loved their new independence. The men had a great time together. They laughed and told jokes and hunted. The women, too, had a wonderful time. While they worked, they told stories and sang and made fun of the men. Sometimes, they would go down to the banks of the river and take off their clothes and tease the men about sex.

As the years passed, the men found they could grow crops easily, without any help from women. But they grew tired of each other, and they longed terribly for the women.

Meanwhile, the women had trouble with their crops. They went hungry. They missed the men terribly.

Both men and women tried to satisfy their physical longings by themselves. The women used bones, cactus, or long, thick stones. The men used warm mud, or raw meat.

Finally, at the end of four years, they were ready to admit that they needed each other and loved each other.

They reunited and promised themselves they would never part again.

CONNECTING THE STORY TO YOUR LIFE

1. When First Woman notices that the people she has brought into the Fourth World look ragged, she feels embarrassed. A little later, the people themselves grow self-conscious about the differences between them and the people who already live in the Fourth World.

What role has embarrassment played in your own life? When have you felt embarrassed about your own looks or behaviors?

What kinds of situations triggered these feelings? Do such situations still occur in your life?

Are these situations related to shaming experiences in childhood? Can you change the situation, and your response to it, by changing your own behavior or attitudes?

2. Feelings are like road maps to our psyches: they remind us of who we really are; they reveal our true selves to us. If the People had noticed their feelings when Coyote tried to convince them to go against their morals and steal, they would have ignored him to begin with.

In the past, it was common to make children feel embarrassed or ashamed of such normal human emotions as anger, resentment, and jealousy. We now know that all our feelings, no matter what they are, are important. How did your family treat feelings? If you have children, how do you respond to their feelings? What unresolved feelings do you still have from childhood?

If you are at a point on your personal journey where you find you still have a hard time admitting your feelings to yourself or acknowledging them to your friends, perform some healing act to help you honor your feelings. Picture yourself as an ancient shaman healing yourself and others. Buy bags of colored sands at a craft shop. In a spirit of reverence and gratitude, remembering the thousands of years of sand painting that have preceded you, make some kind of geometric or abstract sand painting. Follow your intuition about what colors to use where. Or perform whatever type of healing act resonates most for you: plant a flower, sing a song, write a story. Just saying the words "Thank you, feelings, for being there," each morning when you first wake up will alter your perception of your feelings and their role in your life.

3. In the story of Ko-chin-ni-na-ko, Spider Woman took sides: she supported Ko-chin-ni-na-ko against her truly monstrous husband.

By contrast, in this story she appears as a neutral force. When the four volunteers are about to go off and steal corn from the Pueblo Indians, Spider Woman obligingly makes carrying bags for them. It is almost as if she wanted to provide them with the means to learn a lesson they hadn't learned: to stick to their principles even in a difficult situation.

In this respect both Spider Woman and First Woman serve mainly as mentors here. First Woman offers advice, but she doesn't try to force anyone to follow it. Both she and Spider Woman give the people the space to make their own mistakes. When the People are ready to listen to her, First Woman provides more advice. But again she doesn't insist that they follow it.

Who have been the wise mentors in your life? In what ways have they acted like Spider Woman? In what ways have they acted the opposite of Spider Woman?

Have you reached a point where you are able to reach out and mentor others? What have your experiences as a mentor been like? Have you been able to allow the person you mentor the freedom to make his or her own mistakes?

Imagine First Woman as your core mentor. Find a comfortable place to sit quietly and do a visualization in which you take your troubles to First Woman, talk with her, ask her advice, then go out and make your own decisions about your life.

4. Some traditional Navajo people today say that if you see a coyote, it means there is something you are not paying attention to, or some situation or potential problem in your life that you are not seeing in the proper way.

If you have a coyote figure in your house, place it where you will stop and look at it once a day. Then take five minutes to sit with your eyes closed and think about what problems you might not be seeing the right way. Or think about when you might be following Coyote's advice to be lazy or deceitful. Think about the times someone else has convinced you to do something against your better judgment, as Coyote convinced the Dine'é.

5. In many Native American traditions, Coyote is a trickster, or is somehow duplicitous and untrustworthy. Here he is the voice of manipulative thinking. Taking things isn't really stealing, he tells people.

Manipulative people are first cousins to crazymakers. Like crazymakers, they can have a profoundly destructive effect on our lives.

What manipulative people have you encountered? What are your feelings when you think about these people? Are there manipulative people in your life today? These people are your Coyotes. How can you change your life to be free of them?

Picture yourself inside a sacred circle. At the center a sacred fire burns. First Woman has created this circle and built this fire just to protect you and other people who are at your stage of emotional and spiritual development. Imagine Coyote standing near the edge of the circle, wanting to come in. Imagine yourself piling wood on the fire to keep Coyote out.

Chapter Eleven

White Buffalo Woman

A Tale from the Lakota (Sioux)

This tale is unique because traditional Lakota calendars, known as Winter-Counts, date the events in it to a specific year. Some scholars interpret the year as A.D. 1100. Others say A.D. 1540. In any case, for the Lakota, the story has literal historical truth as well as symbolic and spiritual truth.

In one version or another, this story has received more attention in the popular press than all of the other Native American tales about women's power combined. The version presented here is taken primarily from the account of Lone Man, a warrior who fought against Custer in 1876.

Elements of this story are found in the traditions of other Plains tribes and as far away as the tales of the Pueblo Indians of the Southwest. Even today, the Buffalo Mother is the most important figure in the Pueblos' Buffalo Dance; metaphorically, all large game animals are considered to be her children.

Long ago, in the days when the People still lived far to the east of here, along the shores of a great lake, all the bands got together once a year for a big meeting.

Sometimes they gathered in the summer. Sometimes in the fall. Together they celebrated their victories over their enemies. Together they mourned their defeats. Together they discussed ways to protect their land and their hunting grounds. When the meeting ended, they would scatter.

One year, the Sans Arc band left the meeting and drifted westward in search of buffalo and other large game. They planned to dry the meat and save it for the long, cold winter months.

But day after day no buffalo or other game came into view. When they searched the sky, they could see none of the rising streamers of dust that signify the passing of a herd of the sacred animals.

People went hungry. Little children cried because they wanted something to eat, and there was nothing. Old people died. So two young men were chosen to set out looking for buffalo and other animals.

One day as they searched, the two scouts saw a solitary shape approaching. Hoping it might be a buffalo that had strayed from the herd, they moved forward.

As the creature grew close, they were surprised to see a young woman. She wore a fringed buckskin tunic and carried sage sprigs. Her long black hair hung loose, except where she had tied some of it together with a tuft of buffalo hair. Red paint streaked her cheeks.

"The buffalo tribe has sent me," she said. "Return to your people and tell them to erect a lodge for me in the middle of the camp circle."

Even before she spoke, one of the young men realized he was in the presence of someone who was very sacred, very *wakan*. He felt honored and awed.

The other young man scarcely heard the woman speak. All he noticed was her body, and the sensuous curves beneath her buckskin dress. He wanted to touch her. He wanted to lie with her. He stepped toward her.

His companion tried to stop him, and the woman herself warned him to stay back. But either he was so lost in the fantasy that he didn't hear her, or so caught up in his lust that he didn't care. He pushed her to the ground.

All at once, a cloud covered the young man. Some say that from the cloud could be heard the sound of a thousand rattlesnakes.

When the cloud lifted, all that remained were his bones. The young woman was unharmed.

She finished her instructions and told the other young man to return to camp, without looking back.

When the old men heard his story, they ordered the lodge built at once. Just as the woman from the buffalo nation had asked, the door faced east, to greet the rising sun.

Sage was spread all around, and a buffalo skull was placed on a rack.

Soon even the hungriest person in the camp was talking about the mysterious young woman and praying that she would save the People.

The next morning, just as the sun rose, people heard someone singing a song. It went like this:

> *My breath can be seen,*
> *and my voice can be heard*
> *as I walk toward this nation*
> *this buffalo nation.*
> *My breath can be seen*
> *and my voice can be heard*
> *as I bring you this bundle.*
> *This is why I am walking.*
> *This is why I am walking.*

As the song ended, the mystery woman entered the camp. She was dressed as she had been the previous day. But now, instead of sage, she held a long pipe. It had a beautiful red bowl made of carved stone, and the neck of the pipe was curved like the windpipe of a buffalo calf.

The woman entered the new lodge, and the chief greeted her. "All that we have is yours," he said. "Please forgive us. We are so poor that we don't even have any food to offer you. In its place, please accept a drink of rainwater."

He dipped a braid into a buffalo horn filled with rainwater, then handed the dripping grass to her. She sipped.

Then the woman spoke to the people. "Sisters and brothers, we are all one great family, and Wakantanka, the Great Mystery, smiles on us today. Because you are good people, the buffalo tribe has chosen to honor you with this pipe. It is a pipe of peace. A pipe of healing. It stands as a promise that someday you will be at peace permanently, and there will be no more war. Until then, when you make peace with another nation, you will smoke this pipe, and it will be the pledge of your peace."

She also said that when someone was ill, the medicine person could smoke the pipe, and that person would get well. She reminded the people that all good things come from the four directions and from the earth and sky.

She reminded them of the importance of harmony within families.

She spoke to the women in the crowd. "My sisters, without you, there would be no life. You possess the gift of kindness. You know the art of remembering and honoring the dead, long after they are gone."

To the children, she said, "Little sisters and little brothers, you are the most sacred gift of all. Someday this pipe will be yours. Honor it all your lives."

To the men, she said, "My brothers, remember that this pipe is to be used only for good purpose. If you fail to honor what is above, or you disrespect what is below, if you do anything against the four directions, you will suffer. Use this pipe to offer your sacrifices. Smoke this pipe when the People are hungry, and it will bring the buffalo to you."

To the chief she said, "Older brother, by this pipe and with this pipe the tribe will have its life. You have been chosen to be the guardian of the pipe for the People. Honor it. Preserve it. Guard it well."

Then she took a piece of old buffalo chip lying on the earth, held it in the fire, and lit the pipe. With the stem, she motioned toward the sky. "This offering goes to the sky, for all the gifts it gives," she said.

Pointing the pipe stem to the earth, she said, "This offering goes to the earth, for all the gifts it gives."

She pointed to each of the four directions and said, "This offering goes to the four winds, for all the gifts they bring."

Some say she also introduced five sacred ceremonies to the People: the Sun Dance, the Vision Cry, the Buffalo Chant, the Ghost Keeper, and the Foster-Parent Chant.

Following her wishes, people sat quietly and watched her depart. Just at the moment when she stepped out of the tent, she changed into a white buffalo and thundered away.

Since that day, the robe of a white buffalo has been considered sacred. And since that day, the People have followed the teachings of White Buffalo Woman and preserved and honored the sacred pipe.

Even now, anyone who swears by the sacred pipe and does not keep his word will die. It is said that the White man's General Custer swore by the pipe that he would not harm the People. That is why he died; he did not keep his sacred promise.

THE WOMAN WHO BROUGHT BUFFALO TO THE PEOPLE

IN A RELATED STORY FROM THE CHEYENNE PEOPLE, the theme of punishment for selfish sexual longings is absent. Instead, one of the young men becomes the woman's husband; the other takes her as his sister.

With the woman's assistance, the People escape starvation. From the North, she supplies them with corn. From the South, with elk, deer, and other large game animals. From the West she brings birds. From the East come vast herds of buffalo, the first anyone has ever seen.

WOMEN'S SOCIETIES

THE ARRIVAL OF HORSES TO THE PLAINS IN THE 1700s brought major changes to the lives of the Lakota and others. One innovation was an increasing emphasis on male activities and maleness. Even so, many ceremonies and societies continued to honor women.

These included a women's society known as Praiseworthy Women. Before performing a ceremony, members wrapped strips of otterskin around their foreheads and wore eagle feathers in their hair. While a group of men sang for them, the women danced in a circle.

Another group, the Tanners, honored women as teepee makers. When a woman needed to make a teepee cover, she sent a messenger to throw tent-making tools through the doorways of each of the other teepee-makers in the encampment. On the appointed day, the women feasted together and sewed skins provided by their hostess into a new teepee cover.

One of the most sacred and powerful societies of all was the Women's Medicine Cult. Only women who had had certain kinds of dreams of buffalo and other large animals could belong. These dreams gave them the power to forecast success in war during the coming year. It also made them responsible for blessing and protecting young men who were going to war.

The women made the young men war shields and imbued the shields with sacred powers. To each young man the women also gave a small medicine bag with feathers, bird skins, or some other sacred object attached.

CONNECTING THE STORY TO YOUR LIFE

1. In this story a young man dies because he can see the woman only as a sex object, and would have raped her, if he could. As you think back over this part of the story, what feelings come up for you? Remember, whatever they are, they are your feelings, and they are not right or wrong. They are simply road maps that guide you toward a better understanding of yourself.

In thinking back over your own life, what are some of your experiences in being treated as a sex object? Have you ever, consciously or unconsciously, treated someone as a sex object yourself? How do you feel about those experiences today? If you still feel a sense of being poisoned or damaged by these experiences in any way, work through the exercises in one of the many manuals related to sexual healing. One good source book is *The Sexual Healing Journey* by Wendy Maltz. Or, if you'd prefer, paint a painting, write a poem, make a song, or do some other creative project that gives you a feeling of empowerment.

If you have already finished healing from such experiences, do something to honor yourself and your healing process. Make a collage of items that remind you of the steps along the path. Perform a ritual with friends. Or make a new display for your shrine, with items that symbolize and honor your healing. (Never mind whether anyone else would make sense of the objects. The important thing is that they mean something to you.) Or write a poem or song celebrating your victories. Even such a simple act as taking a ritual bath can be a powerful way of honoring your own healing process.

2. Make a diagram of the four directions. Include a place for the sky above and the earth below. Then jot down the names of people, events, or places from your own life that are forces for good and have come to you from one of the four directions or from the sky or earth. These powerful forces may be part of your ordinary life, such as a friend who lives east of you or a beloved aunt who lives north of you. Imagine yourself holding the sacred pipe and blessing each of the four directions in your own life.

If you enjoy making chants, create a chant that honors the forces in each of these directions in turn. Or do some other art project that honors these positive powers in your life.

3. Sit quietly somewhere and let your mind grow still. Visualize White Buffalo Woman appearing to you personally at a time of deep need. Picture yourself treating her with reverence and respect. Imagine her offering you wisdom connected to your own personal life. Visualize what she would tell you about how to deal with the problems on your job. Picture her giving you advice about how to deal with difficult family members. Imagine what she would tell you about any problems you have in relationships.

Write her words down or speak them into a tape recorder, so that you can come back and look at them or hear them again and again.

If you are not already in the habit of doing so, begin listening for the voice of the wise woman inside you. Keep a notebook with you so that you can jot down any messages she gives you before they disappear. (If you'd rather approach this more analytically, consider these as messages from your right brain to your left brain. In either case, write them down quickly, before they disappear.)

4. Imagine that one hundred years from now a girl will be born into your extended family. As she grows up, she will know little or nothing about you. She may not even know that you existed.

Write a long letter in which you tell her about yourself and your life. Share any wisdom that you believe would make her life easier. Share any pains you have had that will help her deal some-day with similar pains. Tell her about whatever matters most to you.

Describe the room in which you are sitting. Tell her what your feelings are as you write to her. Close the letter by giving her your blessings, in whatever manner is most meaningful to you.

Enclose a copy of a favorite photograph of yourself. Put the letter with your will, and ask that it be preserved and handed down from woman to woman in your family until one hundred years have passed, and it can be given to the mother of the young woman to whom you are writing. Choose the age at which you wish her to receive the letter, and ask that it be given to her on her birthday that year.

Chapter Twelve

The Buffalo Wife

A Tale of the Piegan (Blackfeet)

If you have ever been raped, you may wish to skip this story completely. It begins with a rape, and it is far from being a simple story of punishment for bad deeds.

As in most legends, the story is metaphor. Across the northern Great Plains and beyond, various elements from the narrative appear again and again in the traditions of many tribes.

Taken together, the parts of this complex tale portray the many stages in an archetypal relationship, full of bad and good, as the balance of power shifts back and forth. It shows the ways in which the abuse of power hurts, and it reminds us of the destructiveness when one person tries to force his will, or hers, on another.

It also shows the life-restoring power of love, and reminds us that in a good relationship, after all the tests and trials, a day arrives when questions of power and control disappear, and there is only love.

If you are a rape victim and choose to read this story, please pay close attention to your feelings as you read, or read the story aloud with a friend or some other person you trust.

Once there was a beautiful buffalo cow, with long, shining dark fur. One day, as she was grazing with the herd, she got caught in a mud hole, and her companions left her behind.

A thoughtless young man was passing along and saw the buffalo cow, immobile in the mud. He could have freed her. Instead, he raped her. If she had been free, she could have lowered her head and twisted around and gored him with her horns. But there was nothing she could do to stop him.

When the young man finished, he continued on his way as if nothing had happened.

Finally, the buffalo cow was able to pull herself out of the mud and return to the herd. She said nothing to the other buffalos about what had happened. But the next spring, when other cows were giving birth to buffalo calves, she gave birth to a creature that was sometimes a buffalo calf, sometimes a human boy.

As her son grew, he grazed with her across the prairies and hills. But sometimes he would turn into a boy and show up at a human camp and play games with the children there. When the people in the camp asked him who he was, he would shake his head and disappear.

The boy watched the children going into their parents' lodges, and he longed to find his own father. One day he went to his mother, who was grazing in the tall grass, and told her he was going to search for his father.

"Be careful, my son," she cautioned. "Even though you can change your shape and look like them, you come from me. Something bad could happen."

The next time the boy visited a human camp, he stopped at the lodge of the headman and explained that he was searching for his father. The man felt sorry for the fatherless boy, and he called all the old men in the band to come into the camp.

The boy looked the men over, but shook his head. He couldn't believe that his father was one of these old men.

The leader sent for all the middle-aged men, but again the boy looked them over and shook his head.

Now the leader sent for all the young married men, but again the boy looked them over in disappointment. He was sure none was his father.

Finally the chief called all the young unmarried men in. This time, when the boy looked them over, he saw one he believed was his father. He ran to the man, and they embraced. The man had matured since the day he raped the buffalo cow. He accepted the boy as his son, and they lived together in his lodge.

One day the boy invited his father to go out into the countryside to visit his mother. The father agreed.

"When we get close to her, she will run at you and hook your clothes with her horns four times," the boy cautioned. "But you must stand totally still, and nothing bad will happen."

It occurred as the boy had predicted. When they found the buffalo cow, she charged the man four times, and four times he stood motionless as her horns tore his clothes. When the cow rushed forward the final time, she changed into a woman.

The man was happy to see that the buffalo cow had become a woman. He took her home, and she became his wife.

In the first days when she lived in his lodge, the woman warned him, "No matter what happens, you must never hit me."

The man agreed.

Many years passed, and the man and woman lived together happily. She made a good wife, and he had matured enough by now to make a good husband.

Then one day, when the man was feeling unhappy and restless, he invited guests home without telling his wife. When they showed up at her door, she said, "I'm busy. I can't cook for so many people today."

With that, the husband grew angry. He pulled a stick out of the fire and struck her.

At that moment, both his wife and his son vanished. Later, people told him they had seen a buffalo cow and a buffalo calf running through the camp, back out into the countryside.

The husband felt terrible. Again and again he relived those moments. How he wished he hadn't struck his wife. Finally he decided to search for his wife and beg her forgiveness.

In order not to scare the buffalos away, he smeared his arms and legs with mud from the buffalo wallow. Then he traveled night and day until he found the herd. The animals were dancing the Buffalo Dance.

As he stood at a distance and watched, a buffalo calf approached him.

It was his son.

"I have come to take you and your mother home," the man said.

"That will be very difficult," his son said. "You will have to pass many tests. You will have to prove to the chief of the buffalos that you can recognize me."

The man stared at him. The boy looked exactly like every other buffalo calf.

"When the buffalo calves pass in front of you, I will hold up my tail," the son said. "That's how you'll know it's me."

Just as the son had predicted, the buffalo chief required the man to pick the calf he believed to be his son out of the herd. As the calves passed in front of him, the son raised his tail, and the man was able to identify his son.

But the buffalo chief wasn't satisfied. "You will have to identify your son four times," he said.

The next time, the son told his father he would close one eye, and the father again knew his son.

The third time, the son told his father he would droop one ear down as a signal, and again the father selected his son.

The final time, the son told his father he would dance on three legs, and wave his fourth leg in the air.

This time, when the calves came in front of the man, one of the other calves saw the son dancing with a leg in the air. It looked to him like some kind of new fancy dance. So he put his leg up, too.

The man saw both calves dancing with a leg in the air and chose the wrong calf as his son.

Instantly, the herd of buffalos rushed forward and trampled the man to death. Their hooves pressed him completely into the ground.

Then all the buffalos ran away except for the mother, the son, and an old bull.

For some time, the three mourned the death of the man. But then one day they found a small bone that had not been ground into the dust. They took the bone into a sweat house, and, after many ceremonies, the man was restored to life.

At that moment, the calf-boy and his mother turned back into human beings and went back with the man to his tribe. With the songs and dances he had learned among the buffalo, the man became the founder of the Bull Society and the Horn Society, and his wife became the founder of the women's societies.

THE KIDNAPPED MOTHER

IN A TALE FROM THE TEWA-SPEAKING PUEBLO INdians, White Corn Woman is a widow and the mother of two sons, both named Fire. The Sun wants to marry White Corn Woman. So does Faint Star.

White Corn Woman refuses both would-be husbands. So Faint Star kidnaps her. Then the Sun steals her from Faint Star. Finally Spider Old Woman helps the two Fires rescue their mother and bring her safely home.

On the surface, this story relates to a woman's right to choose the kind of male energy she allows into her life. On a deeper level, it suggests that for some women the best male energy is already inside them—symbolized by White Corn Woman's two sons.

CONNECTING THE STORY TO YOUR LIFE

A literal, non-Indian interpretation of this story would produce a horrifying story line: man rapes innocent victim. She later marries him. He acts brutal again, so she disappears. In their next encounter, she restores him to life. Because of what he has learned from her, he becomes powerful and famous.

That is precisely the kind of true-life story that feminists have been railing against, with justification, for decades. But "The Buffalo Wife" isn't a literal story. It's metaphor. Nowhere does the narrative justify or excuse the man's actions. It simply presents them as they are: a prelude to healing and redemption.

Among her many symbolic meanings, the buffalo wife stands for the forces of nature. Like nature, she is nonjudgmental. But certain laws govern her conduct. In the end, as the man relates to her in increasingly mature ways, his connection to her becomes the vehicle through which he reaches fulfillment, wisdom, and enlightenment.

In that respect, this story is an allegory for our times. As we have been reminded repeatedly in the past half century, all of us on the planet, male or female, must rethink and redefine our connection with nature, or face mass destruction.

1. If you can conveniently do so, take a trip into a wilderness area and spend time getting reconnected to nature. While you are alone with nature, do a mini life review. What role has nature played in your life so far? What role would you like it to play in the future?

During your time in the wilderness, and afterward, pay particular attention to your dreams. What animals appear in them? What do these animals mean to you?

In many Native American traditions, animals are considered more evolved spiritually than humans: they are a link between humans and the gods. In what way might the animals in your dreams be a link between your everyday self and your higher self?

Create a poem, chant, or other narrative in which you are sometimes the animal in your dreams, sometimes your everyday self.

2. Have there been points in your life when you have acted mindlessly and been destructively self-centered at the expense of other people? What were the consequences of your actions? How have you grown since then?

Create some kind of healing ritual that you can perform alone or with friends, symbolizing your movement toward a sense of connection with and caring for all beings everywhere.

3. It would be hard to think of a better symbol for the completely innocent victim than the buffalo cow trapped alone in the mud. But she doesn't remain a victim. Time, a return to her roots (the buffalo nation), and a strong connection with nature help her heal.

Looking back over your own life, what situations, sexual or nonsexual, have you felt victimized in? How did you heal? What steps do you still need to take in order to finish healing?

4. The first time the man acts brutally toward the buffalo cow, she is helpless: she is all alone, trapped in the mud, and unable to escape.

Years later, the second time he begins to act brutally toward her, she has resources. She responds by disappearing.

Have there been times in your own life when the only way to deal with a difficult person you were close to was to disappear? Close your eyes and sit in a quiet place and think about those times. What was the outcome each time? Are you still out of contact with this person? Are you comfortable with the situation as it is today?

5. Create a narrative of your own life, focusing on the stages of spiritual and emotional evolution you have undergone so far. What were the catalysts to change? What stages do you envision still ahead for yourself? Include these in your narrative. Portray yourself at the end of your life as wise, complex, full of dignity and hope, passing on your accumulated knowledge to others.

6. If you could start a spiritual society similar to the ones the man and his buffalo wife establish at the end of this story, who would be the members? What would be the rituals and ceremonies? Picture yourself as an inhabitant of the Americas a thousand years ago, returning to your people after a journey of self-discovery. Picture yourself founding sacred societies.

Chapter Thirteen

Sweet Corn Woman's Tale

A Story of the Tewa

In the Tewa-speaking Pueblo Indian villages of northern New Mexico, traditional tales are full of powerful female figures. These include Summer Mother and Winter Mother, the mothers of all humankind. They include Spider Old Woman Grandmother. They include a generic mother figure, known simply as Our Mother. And they include many women with human flaws and failings. In this story jealousy and envy disrupt many lives.

Once, long ago, a man named Shell Flower lived with his mother and father, Shriveled Corn Old Woman and Shriveled Corn Old Man. Shell Flower was a good hunter, and he brought many deer back to the village for his parents to eat. Sometimes in the late mornings when he returned with a deer, the young women of the village would watch him and say, "I wonder which one of us Shell Flower is going to marry." Each one wanted Shell Flower for herself.

Soon the women's longing for Shell Flower turned into a competition.

The young woman named Blue Corn went first. Humming happily, she spent a whole afternoon grinding the finest kernels of blue corn into a perfect cornmeal. The next day she filled her basket and brought it to Shell Flower's house.

Shell Flower thanked her, but he was not impressed.

The following day the young woman named Yellow Corn watched for Shell Flower's return. Then she walked to his house and presented him with a basket full of finely ground yellow corn.

He thanked her, too, but again there was nothing about Yellow Corn or her gift that made him desire her.

The same thing happened the following morning to Red Corn and the following morning to White Corn. After that, Speckled Corn tried, but again, Shell Flower was not impressed.

Each time, Shell Flower treated the young women politely. But they could see he was not interested in any of them.

"What does this man want?" they complained among themselves as they sat grinding corn together in the house they shared. "We are beautiful. We are good people. We grind the finest cornmeal. What's wrong with him? Why doesn't he want us?"

Meanwhile another young woman, Sweet Corn, who lived all by herself, was watching what happened. She noticed that all the other young women were so busy thinking about how much they wanted Shell Flower that they scarcely saw him as a separate person with his own wants and needs.

Sweet Corn decided to wait until she saw Shell Flower coming home, before grinding some fresh cornmeal of her own.

She did that. Then she went to Shell Flower's house and offered him the fresh cornmeal.

"But this looks so fresh," he said. "When did you grind it?"

"Just now, as I was watching you come home with your deer," she replied.

Then Shell Flower understood that Sweet Corn saw him for who he was, and he fell in love with her. "You are the one I want for my wife," he said.

Shell Flower and Sweet Corn married, and they were very happy.

But the other Corn Women felt betrayed. They were angry that Sweet Corn, a woman they'd never much cared for anyway, got the husband they wanted.

One morning early, just as Shell Flower was leaving on the hunt, they walked to Sweet Corn's house and said to her, "Sister, why don't you come with us? Bring a big basket of corn, and we'll help you grind it."

Sweet Corn went with them, but after a while, Blue Corn suggested they should stop working and play a game.

"I don't want to do that. I'm ready to go home," Sweet Corn said.

The other Corn Women made fun of her. "Just stay long enough to play this hoop game with us," they said.

"Okay, but as soon as we're done, I'm going straight home," she replied.

"I'll throw the hoop," said Blue Corn. "If you can catch it and put your hand through it, it's yours."

When Sweet Corn put her hand through the hoop, she changed all at once into a white-tailed fox. The other Corn Women laughed and threw stones at her. "Now there's nothing you can do. Now Shell Flower will want us, and we can live with him," they taunted.

Sweet Corn didn't know what to do, so she walked out to meet Shell Flower as he was returning home.

"I wonder why this little fox is following me," Shell Flower asked himself. "Maybe she's hungry." He cut some meat off the deer and threw it to her.

But even though she now had the body of an animal, Sweet Corn couldn't bear to eat raw meat. She just continued to follow Shell Flower, until they reached home, and the dogs, not recognizing her, chased her away.

When Shell Flower found the house empty, he wondered what had happened to Sweet Corn. He put the deer down and waited. Then he remembered the other Corn Women had come to his house that morning, so he went to ask them.

"Oh, she left and went home," Blue Corn told him. "We don't have any idea where she might be." The Corn Women laughed to themselves. After all, that was the truth, wasn't it? She had left. She had gone home. But the dogs had chased her away, and now they didn't know where the fox had gone.

For days, Shell Flower lay in his house, grieving because Sweet Corn had disappeared. He roused himself only to send out emissaries in each of the four directions to tell people the story of his missing wife and ask for news of her.

"What is wrong with that man?" the other Corn Women asked themselves. "We are better than Sweet Corn. But he just lies there grieving in the wind and cold and heat." They dressed up in their best clothes and passed right outside his house, laughing and calling to each other so that he couldn't fail to notice them.

Shell Flower ignored them. All he could think of was Sweet Corn and how much he missed her and how worried he was about her.

Meanwhile the little fox was growing thinner and thinner from not eating and from worrying about Shell Flower. It made her so sad to see how Shell Flower grieved, that she decided to go far away to the East, where the Comanches and Kiowas lived.

Even far away, she could never get her husband out of her mind. So finally she returned home. She could get just close enough to see that Shell Flower was still lying there, so thin he was almost dead, before the dogs drove her away.

She went to the South. There she fell into a trap made by Prayer Stick Old Man, who was too old to hunt and killed foxes for himself and his wife to use for food and clothing.

The next morning Prayer Stick looked into the pit and saw the fox crying.

"That's strange," said Prayer Stick Old Man. "Usually foxes don't cry." He picked up a stick and was about to kill her, the way he killed all foxes, by hitting her on the back of the neck, but the fox ignored him and continued to cry. Then he remembered the story of the disappearance of Shell Flower's wife.

"Are you Sweet Corn Woman?" he asked.

Because she was a fox, Sweet Corn could not speak. She only nodded.

"You're sure this isn't just some kind of trick?" Prayer Stick Old Man asked.

The little fox shook her head. So Prayer Stick Old Man took her home to his wife, Prayer Stick Old Woman. Carefully they examined the animal, searching through the hairs on the top of her head for the magic place that held the key to her enchantment. Finally they found what they were looking for. It was a little spot, hard and round, that resembled a pin. They pulled at it, and her skin came off.

This broke the spell. Sweet Corn was a woman again. But she had no clothes, and she was ragged and smelly. Together the old man and the old woman bathed her. Then they gave her clothes and food.

"Do you know what saved you?" the old couple asked. Sweet Corn shook her head.

"Nothing that happened was your husband's fault, but some women would have blamed him anyway. Because you thought only good things about him, you have survived."

Before Sweet Corn left, Prayer Stick Old Man made her a special hoop. "The other Corn Women will be jealous of you again," he said. "They will want this hoop. Act like you don't want them to touch it. Then roll it on the ground, and say, 'Whoever catches it first, that person can have it.' "

When Sweet Corn reached her old home, she found Shell Flower too weak to talk or stand up. The buffalo robe he lay under had grown so old during his long months of mourning that all the hairs had blown off. But when he saw Sweet Corn, it made him so happy that he recovered quickly.

Meanwhile, the other Corn Women saw her and said, "Oh, sister, where have you been? We missed you."

"I was just out walking," she said.

They noticed the new hoop tied to her belt. "Give us your new hoop. After all, aren't we all sisters?" they said.

"I'm giving this to no one," Sweet Corn replied.

The other Corn Women kept pestering her.

Finally she untied the hoop from her belt and rolled it toward them. "Whoever catches it first, that person can have it."

One of the Corn Women grabbed it, and they all turned into

snakes. "Because you do not know how to love, you will crawl on the ground," she said. Then she picked up the hoop and went home.

After that, Sweet Corn and Shell Flower lived happily for many years, and no one ever bothered them again.

BRINGING THE DEAD TO LIFE

 AROUND THE COUNTRY, TRADI-tional stories include the theme of bringing the dead back to life. As in the story "The Buffalo Wife," some part of the dead person or some possession of the dead person is required in order to restore life.

In one Winnebago story, Wash-ching-geka, the Son of the Earth Maker, is murdered by a monster who would have eaten him, except that he didn't taste good. Holding what remains of him, his grandmother brings him back to life.

In a story from the Tiwa-speaking Pueblo of Isleta similar to "Sweet Corn Woman's Tale," jealous women murder a woman who is also the moon. When her husband finally discovers where they have buried her body, he sends a bird to bring back a white flower that is growing from her grave. From this flower he is able to restore his beloved wife to life.

CONNECTING THE STORY TO YOUR LIFE

1. As you read this story, what feelings come up for you? Have there been times in your life when you suffered because of someone else's jealousy of you? How do you feel about the experience

now? Make a narrative of your own life that recounts these experiences in story form. Or make an arrangement of objects on
your shrine that remind you of the events. If you have not finished
healing from these events, create a chant, a song, or a series of
affirmations that help you feel more empowered.

2. In being transformed into a fox, Sweet Corn loses the ability
to communicate with human beings, and particularly with her husband, Shell Flower. Have there been times in your own life when
you felt emotionally cut off from people you love or unable to
communicate with them? How did the distancing occur? What was
the outcome of the situation?

Is there someone you love whom you feel emotionally cut off
from now? What steps can you take to come back into closer
touch with this person? If you are ready to take those steps, begin
now.

3. Sweet Corn's rescuers, Prayer Stick Old Man and Prayer Stick
Old Woman, represent the wisdom and insight that comes with
age. They are the first human beings who think to ask if the
emaciated little fox is anything other than a fox. And they know
the arcane process whereby Sweet Corn can be released from the
spell. In bathing her, they are symbolically transferring their wisdom to her.

Do you know a man over seventy and a woman over seventy
who represent wisdom and insight to you? What wisdom and
blessings have you already gained from these people? What transformations or reconnections have they helped you with in your
life? If you would like to spend more time with them than you
currently do, think of three ways in which you could rearrange
your life to do so, and implement one of them.

Make a song or a poem that honors the wisdom that comes
with age.

4. The jealous Corn Women can see Shell Flower only as an extension of themselves. They cannot see him as a separate person. What experiences in your own life have helped you see yourself more clearly as a separate person? Are there ways in which you would like to improve your sense of yourself as a separate person?

If so, sit quietly and let your mind float for a while. Then visualize yourself in a variety of settings. When do you feel most yourself, most centered and whole? When do you feel most fragile, least able to maintain your identity as a separate person? If you're not sure, then keep a small notebook with you for the next two weeks and watch your feelings and responses to the world. Make notes about the times you feel most centered and whole, and the times you feel most vulnerable.

What changes do you need to make in your own attitudes, or in your environment, to increase the number of situations when you are able to feel happy and whole as a separate person?

5. One theme in this story is the damage that occurs when women don't support each other. Which of the women in your own life are the most supportive and nurturing? Which are the most difficult? Are there women in your life whom you don't trust? If so, what changes can you make so that these people are no longer in your life? If it isn't practical to eliminate them from your life, what can you do to provide a circle of safety around yourself, to reduce the effect of their poison?

How can you rearrange your life to spend more time with the women whom you find most supportive and nurturing?

6. Sacred circles and sacred hoops have different meanings in different cultures and different tales. In many Pueblo tales, the hoop is a vehicle of metamorphosis, a means whereby human beings can pass from a human form to an animal form and back, sometimes willingly, sometimes unwillingly. Sometimes the sacred hoop is linked to Spider Old Woman and her power.

Make a sacred hoop for yourself, or buy a hoop at a craft store and decorate it in a way that is meaningful to you. Holding the hoop, do a visualization about yourself as the animal that came to you in the previous chapter's exercises (see page 111).

Imagine yourself going back and forth through the hoop, passing from human form to animal and back again. Or, if you'd rather, imagine the hoop as the vehicle through which you can make future transformations in your life.

Chapter Fourteen

The Women Warriors

A Tale from the Tewa Pueblos

For the past fifty years we, as a culture, have focused much attention on the question of what happens when women refuse to follow expected roles. Like the women in this story, some contemporary women have found themselves punished in various ways for their choices. But with the help of Spider Woman, these two ancient women turn a difficult situation into a time of transformation and empowerment.

Once, long ago, in a village far away, all the men went off to war. All the wives and mothers stayed home, worrying, crying, praying, and performing rituals so that their men would return safely.

In that village there were two sisters who had never married. The sisters were concerned about the war, of course, and they were sad because their own brothers and nephews were off fighting. But, still, the war didn't affect them the way it affected the other women, whose husbands and sons were fighting.

That made the Outside Cacique, who was in charge of affairs beyond the kiva, angry. He was already annoyed with them because neither had agreed to marry any of the men who wanted them as wives.

"So," he said to the two sisters one day, "you don't want to marry. I guess that must mean you aren't women. And if you aren't women, you must be men. And if you're men, you have to go to war."

The women cried. They were terrified. That made the Outside Cacique angrier. "I'll give you four days to get your bows and arrows ready," he shouted. "After that, you go to war or you die."

The women borrowed bows and arrows. An old man showed them the basic principles of how to shoot, and in four days they set out to join the other warriors.

The war was some distance away. As the women journeyed, they came to Grandmother Spider's house.

"Welcome, daughters," Spider Old Woman said. "Why do you look so sad?"

"We are women, and we know nothing about war," they told her. "Can you help us?"

"I know very little about war, either," Spider Old Woman said. "But I know one thing. You need to give yourselves more time. Wait until tomorrow. I will help you the best I can."

The next day, Spider Old Woman gave them this song:

> *Once we were two sisters.*
> *Once we were two women.*
> *Now we have become Dark Star Man,*
> *Morning Star Man,*
> *Who helps the people in time of war.*
>
> *Once we were two sisters.*
> *Now we are Dark Star Man.*

Spider Old Woman also gave them powerful medicine from plants. "Chew this well, and spit it all over your bodies and all over your bows and arrows. That will keep you safe."

They chewed the medicine. They spit it on themselves and on their weapons and smeared it around. Then they went to war.

They were the bravest warriors there. They killed many enemy men and cut off their scalps as trophies.

On the way home, they stopped in to thank Spider Old Woman. "When you approach your village, you must sing again," she said.

When they were close enough for the people inside the village to hear, they sang,

> *"Once we were two sisters.*
> *Once we were two sisters.*
> *Now we are the Morning Star.*
> *Now we are Dark Star Man."*

The leader of the kiva, the sacred ceremonial chamber, came running out and invited them to enter the kiva as special guests. Then he called all the men together and the women told their stories. They started at the beginning and went on to the very end.

When they had finished, the sisters asked the Summer Cacique, who is the leader of the Summer People, "Did we do the right thing?"

"Yes, my daughters, you did the right thing," the Summer Cacique replied.

"Did we do the right thing?" the sisters asked the Winter Cacique.

"Yes, my daughters, you did the right thing," the leader of the Winter People replied.

The Outside Cacique was silent. He didn't know what to say. Those women were braver than he was.

The men of the village brought the women food. For four days the women sat in the kiva. Then the whole village threw a great feast and danced a scalp dance in their honor.

It may have been then, if not long before that, that the saying began which we all use today, when we want to help people have courage, or find the wisdom that is inside them: "Be a woman. Be a man."

MAKAHTA, WOMAN WARRIOR

IN A LAKOTA (SIOUX) LEGEND, A LEADER OF THE People loses all three sons in battle with Crow warriors. Only a daughter, Makahta, remains.

Many men desire Makahta, but she refuses to marry.

During a time of great turbulence, Makahta decides to go to war herself to avenge her brothers and help her people. Two suitors go with her, a dashing warrior named Red Horn and a shy young man named Little Eagle.

Makahta fights the Crow bravely, but her horse is killed. Red Horn rides right past her, but Little Eagle rushes over and gives her his horse. She begs him to escape, but he knows the horse is not strong enough for two. He whacks it to make it gallop away and take her to safety. Then he dies in battle.

Makahta marries Little Eagle posthumously and mourns him for the rest of her life.

A WARRIOR'S SONG

IN THE IROQUOIS CONfederacy, it was men who went to war, but women who decided when to make war, and when to keep the peace.

In general, across the continent, it was unusual for women to fight in battle. But throughout the centuries, a few Native American women picked up lances or bows and fought alongside the men of their tribe. In the 1700s a Cherokee woman warrior earned the name Da'nawa-gasta, Sharp War, for her bravery in battle. In Arizona in the 1870s, an Apache woman named Lozen was one of the most powerful warriors of her era. Again and again she saved lives, rallied her people, and outwitted invading non-Indians.

Although "A Warrior's Song" comes from the Omaha Indians of the Great Plains, it could easily have been sung by a woman warrior like Lozen or Da'nawa-gasta.

> I will disappear.
> I will not exist.
> But the land where my feet walk,
> It will be here always.
> It will never change.

CONNECTING THE STORY TO YOUR LIFE

1. Envision yourself as a woman warrior a thousand years ago. Why did you go to war? Did you choose to go to war, or did someone else force you to? Did you survive? Did you die fighting? How did you feel when you had to kill?

Create a story or a poem that expresses your feelings or that recounts your exploits. Or write some affirmations about your own powers as a woman warrior. (For instance: I am a warrior. I am a woman warrior. I carry the power of Spider Woman within me. I can do what I have to do.)

2. The metaphors and characters in this story lend themselves well to the imagery and experiences of the workplace. Recast this tale in your mind as a story about the workplace. In this version, you have a job you're perfectly happy with, but your boss doesn't like what you're doing. He requires you to accept a transfer to a place you don't like or to do a kind of work you aren't comfortable doing. How do you respond to this situation?

If you have had experiences in the workplace similar to this, how did they affect you? What were your feelings? How did the situation resolve itself? Were you able to emerge triumphant like the two sisters?

If you are having problems at work now, what are they? Pick the ones that seem most pressing to you and write out plans for changing them: a thirty-day plan, a six-month plan, a one-year plan. Hang these somewhere prominent, or keep them with your journal. Write reports of your progress in your journal.

3. This story is also about the conflict between a woman's right to choose her own roles for herself and the demands society makes on her. Have you been in situations where your own needs and interests didn't conform to the expectations and demands of those around you? How did these situations resolve themselves? What techniques and tools have you developed for protecting yourself against the demands and expectations of others? What techniques have you developed for making decisions about when to adapt to those demands and when to resist?

4. It is still common among traditional residents of the Tewa-speaking Pueblos to give the ritual advice, "Be a woman. Be a man."

In Jungian terms, the advice relates to the need of all of us, men and women, to integrate the male and female aspects of ourselves. Looking at your own life, what stage are you at in balancing and integrating the male and female components of yourself? What are some of the steps still ahead of you? If you are comfortable doing so, ask a close friend who knows you well what steps he or she envisions for you in order to complete this important process.

Harville Hendrix, a psychologist who specializes in the underlying mechanisms of relationships, believes that one principle operating when we are attracted to a certain person as a love object is that we see in that person the missing, cut-off, rejected, or unacknowledged parts of ourselves.

Thinking of your own life, do you see a pattern in the people you feel most strongly drawn to? Can you identify some missing or cut-off part of yourself related to that attraction?

Make a list of five ways you could reintegrate this missing part of yourself back into your own life. Make a six-month plan, a one-year plan, and a five-year plan for achieving this. Or read one of Hendrix's books (*Keeping the Love You Find: A Guide for Singles* or *Getting the Love You Want: A Guide for Couples*) and do the exercises in it.

5. Initially the women in this story are being punished for not having married. If you are single, are there ways in which you feel your family, friends, or society has punished you for being single? What other prices have you paid for remaining single? If you feel empowered as a single person, what are the sources of that empowerment?

When, as a single person, do you feel most centered, most empowered, most grateful to be who you are?

If you sometimes feel disempowered as a single person, what are the sources of that disempowerment? When, as a single person, do you feel least centered, least empowered?

When do you most long to stop being single?

If you are married, have there been times when you felt disempowered, ostracized, or punished for being married? Write about the situation in your journal, or talk these experiences over with your spouse or a trusted friend. When do you feel most empowered, most centered as a married person?

6. The first advice Spider Old Woman gives the two sisters in this tale is to take more time. If you feel pressured in your own life, what are ways in which you can give yourself more time, particularly during periods of transition?

Spider Old Woman also gives the women a song to sing as a way of protecting and empowering themselves. Songs have spiritual and symbolic power, but they also have a practical effect: they are a way of putting us in touch with the nonverbal side of ourselves, with our emotions, with our right brain.

What songs in your own life have special meaning to you, or seem to protect you? What type of music makes you feel most at peace, most yourself, or most fulfilled? Treat yourself to a CD that contains music that you find especially invigorating or empowering.

Chapter Fifteen

Coyote Marries His Daughter

A Northern Ute Tale

This tale of incest shows the horrible price women sometimes pay for trusting their own family members. It shows that since ancient times, some Native Americans have associated self-mutilation with sexual abuse, much as psychologists do today. And it shows that women have the power and the right to take a stand against incest and protect themselves from it.

Whether or not you have personally been the victim of incest, this story is likely to produce a strong emotional response in you. Record these responses carefully.

Coyote could have been happy. He lived in a fine wickiup covered with earth and skins. He had a happy, devoted wife who dug roots and gathered grasshoppers, ants, and grass seeds for the family to eat. He had a beautiful daughter and a happy little boy.

But Coyote wanted more. He looked at his daughter's smooth, glowing skin as she wove baskets, sewed buckskin clothes, and did quillwork. He looked at her long, shining black hair and the curves developing under her clothes, and he lusted after her.

Coyote knew that no matter how devoted his wife was to him, she would never let him touch their daughter. He also knew that their summer camp and their winter shelter both belonged to his wife, just as all homes are owned by the wives. If she found out what he was thinking, he would be condemned to wander forever.

Early one morning Coyote got up and stood in the doorway, facing the rising sun. Then he walked away from home, toward the distant mountain where the family moved each summer. When he was sure that neither his wife nor his son nor his daughter had followed him, he picked up a sharp rock and made long, ugly cuts on his arms and legs. To make the wounds look even worse than they were, he daubed them with dirt and pitch.

For several days he waited. Then he staggered back to his wife's shelter.

"My enemies have tried to kill me," he said. "I am about to die. Make a brush shelter and place me in it, so that I may die in peace."

Coyote's wife and children hurried to do everything as he had said.

When he lay in the shelter, Coyote told his wife, "I have seen a vision. After I am dead, a man will appear, wearing a mountain lion skin. This man is better than all the others. He is the man who must marry our daughter." His wife promised to do as he said.

Coyote lay very still a long time, and they thought he was already dead. But he roused himself once more and whispered, "After I am dead, make a huge pile of brush, so that you can burn my body. But whatever you do, don't look back, because the sight would kill you."

He lay so still and lifeless for so long that his wife decided he was dead. So she and the children heaped up a huge pile of brush. They carried Coyote's corpse over, set it on the brush, and lit fire all around.

"Don't look back," his widow cautioned her children as they hurried away.

But the little boy disobeyed. "Mother, wait!" he cried. "Our father has rolled off the brush. He is crawling away from the fire."

"Shush," said the frightened woman. "Don't you remember what your father said? If you look back, you will die."

"But I tell you, father is crawling away," the little boy repeated. Neither the mother nor the daughter paid any attention, and after a while even the little boy doubted that he had seen what he thought he saw.

All winter long, as they sat by the fire, the mother, son, and daughter mourned the death of Coyote. There was no one to hunt deer for them, and they were often hungry. Spring came, and they moved to their summer camp in the mountains, where they made a fresh brush shelter.

One day, while the daughter was out gathering pine nuts and the mother was sitting by the shelter grinding grass seeds, a man appeared. He wore a mountain lion skin. The long tail of the mountain lion dragged on the ground behind him.

Coyote's widow looked at the man. This was clearly the man from her husband's vision. "That man will be your new brother-in-law," she said to her son. "Go bring him into the camp."

When the young woman returned with the pine nuts, her mother married her to the man in the mountain lion skin. That night they lay together.

The next morning, the mother said to the little boy, "Take your brother-in-law out to hunt squirrels."

The young woman was relieved when they left. She felt confused and uncomfortable around this stranger who was now her husband.

As the man and the boy hunted for squirrels, the boy walked ahead. He held a stick, and when he reached a squirrel hole, he poked the stick into the hole. He shook the stick hard, then pulled it out, and if a squirrel was inside, it would come running out.

But when the first squirrel appeared, instead of using a bow and arrow to kill it, his sister's new husband grabbed the animal with his mouth.

This made the boy suspicious.

Then he noticed that his new brother-in-law went ahead of him and easily found more squirrel holes, as if he already knew the best hunting places. That made the boy even more suspicious.

The boy remembered that his father had had decorative marks on his teeth. One represented his wife, one his son, and one his daughter.

So the boy took his new brother-in-law to a hole that looked like a squirrel hole, but passed all the way through the rock. From one side of the hole, the boy peered through and saw the man standing on the other side, with his mouth wide open, waiting to catch a squirrel.

The boy looked at the man's teeth. There was the mark that represented his mother. There was the mark that represented his sister. There was the mark that represented the boy himself.

The boy pushed his stick into the hole and shook it hard, so that it rattled just like always. He propped it in the hole, so that the wind would continue to rattle it. Then he ran home.

"I told you father didn't die," he said to his mother. Then he reported what he had seen.

At first the mother didn't believe it could be possible. "What did your new husband do with you last night?" she asked her daughter. Her daughter told her the exact details of how they had made love.

The mother went into shock. "That's your father, all right," she said. "That's exactly how he makes love to me."

Both the mother and the daughter felt as if someone had killed them, and they had become ghosts.

When they could finally talk again, they discussed what they could do to escape this terrible evil.

Finally they decided to disappear underneath the ground so that Coyote couldn't find them.

They traveled underground for a long time, before returning to the earth's surface. Still they worried that Coyote would find them, so they floated up into the sky, where they became stars.

Meanwhile, Coyote was still standing at the hole in the rock, waiting for a squirrel to come out. "Shake harder. I'm hungry," he called. But the wind continued to shake the stick with the same slow rhythm as before. Only much later did Coyote notice that his son had disappeared.

Coyote rushed home to his family's camp. "You cannot escape me!" he screamed, but the brush shelter was empty and the fire cold.

Coyote followed the tracks until they disappeared.

Meanwhile, in the heavens, the little boy who had become a star was still just a little boy at heart. He felt lonely for his father. "It would be so nice if my father would see me," he thought.

For a long time, Coyote searched for his family, until one night he looked up and saw that his daughter, his wife, and his son had turned into stars. He cursed and shouted, "Why are you in the sky? Why have you become stars?"

His wife called back, "It is you who have done this. From now on, we will be above, and you will be below. People will call you Coyote. In the earliest morning, you will hunt mice. And when there is a fire in the grass, you will eat the mice as they try to escape. But at night you will raise your face to the stars and see us and howl in grief. You will be called Coyote. And you will never be able to hurt us again."

INCEST

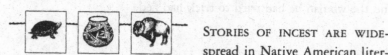

STORIES OF INCEST ARE WIDE-spread in Native American literature. Typically the incest, once discovered, is viewed with horror. Usually the incest is punished, one way or another. In a Yavapai story similar to "Coyote Marries His Daughter," mother and daughter refuse to run away, leave their home, or give up their lives. Instead, they simply kill the incestuous father.

Reflecting real life, the perpetrators in legends may be women as well as men. In one Lakota story from the Great Plains, a young married woman takes her nephew as her lover. In another, a young woman tricks her brother into making love to her. In the end, the victims escape and the perpetrators die.

SLEEPING WITH A LOG

STORYTELLERS AMONG THE IOWA PEOPLE TELL OF A trickster who saw a woman traveling alone. He wanted to seduce her, but he knew she wouldn't speak to a man she didn't know. So he dressed as a woman and traveled with her.

The day passed without her discovering the deception. But that night, when they made camp and went to bed, the trickster tried to make love to her. She pretended to be asleep already, and kept rolling away. Finally he wore out and fell asleep himself, still holding his arms out as if to embrace her.

Quietly the woman got up and found a rotten log full of ants. She carried it over and put it in his arms. In his sleep, he imagined the log was the woman, and he nestled close to it.

The ants bit him, but he thought it was the woman, playing love games. By the time he finally woke up, he was covered with bites, and the woman he had tried to trick had fled.

CONNECTING THE STORY TO YOUR LIFE

Incest is one of the most difficult and damaging of all human experiences. Families in which incest is present may show a polished exterior to the world, but in private they are usually deeply dysfunctional. The incest is seldom the only form of abuse: verbal abuse and physical (nonsexual) cruelty are also common. Members of such families are almost always heavily into denial, not just about the incest, but about many aspects of life.

1. No matter what your age, if you are now in a situation in which you are being sexually abused in any way, or if you know of someone who is in such a situation, please put this book down right now and call your local Rape Crisis Center. Allies, safety, and protection are only a phone call away.

If you have been the victim of incest or any other kind of sexual abuse and have not yet had the help of a trained therapist in working through the effects of the experience, the Rape Crisis Center or similar community agencies can help you obtain affordable counseling.

If you have been fortunate enough not to experience incest directly, consider reaching out to those who have. Volunteer at your local Rape Crisis Center or a similar agency. Provide a safe, nonjudgmental, listening ear to friends who have had such experiences. Encourage those who need it to seek professional help.

Like incest, self-mutilation is an unpleasant and frightening topic. In the story, it is the rapist who mutilates himself. More typically, it is the victim, usually a teenager. If you know someone who has talked about self-mutilation, or acted on it, help that person find professional help. If you have had impulses to cut yourself or otherwise harm yourself, see a therapist at once.

In experiences you have had with incest, or experiences of people you know, what are the common themes?

2. If you are comfortable doing so, go back through the story and imagine yourself in the role of the mother. Focus on your feelings: disbelief, horror, anger, fear, self-blame, determination to create safety for yourself and your children. Visualize yourself as an ancient medicine woman, performing a healing ritual for the mother before she ascends to the sky. Visualize yourself singing chants to heal her.

3. If you are comfortable doing so, go back through the story and imagine yourself as the brother. Again, concentrate on your feelings, whatever they might be: anger, resentment, disgust, confusion. Visualize yourself as an ancient medicine woman, performing a healing ritual for the brother. Visualize yourself giving the brother a dream that will heal him and guide him in his new life as a star.

4. If you are comfortable doing so, go back through the story and visualize yourself as the daughter, the incest victim. Once more, concentrate on your feelings, whatever they are: helplessness, disgust, anguish, perhaps even self-loathing (a common response of incest and other rape victims). Once more, visualize yourself as an ancient medicine woman, this time performing a healing ritual for the daughter. Give her a ritual bath in sacred corn pollen. Draw a sacred circle around her to protect her. Make a sand painting of geometric or abstract images to symbolize the healing process. What words would you speak to her?

5. Like characters in earlier stories, the wife, daughter, and son escape this difficult situation by vanishing. Ultimately they cut themselves off permanently from the villain. Although he can see them, they are safe now. There is no way he will ever be able to hurt any of them again.

Create a new display on your shrine. Place objects on it that to you symbolize healing from your deepest traumas, whatever they might be. Or do a visualization in which you picture yourself joining the stars and becoming safe for all time.

Chapter Sixteen

The Abandoned Children

A Story from the White Clay People (Gros Ventre)

On the surface, this story begins with the tragedies that follow parental brutality. As metaphor, it recounts the child's passage from innocence to independence. It also reminds us that people who have abandoned the child within die a terrible spiritual death—and that miracles happen when the male and female within us work together. Like the children in the story, we survive and thrive.

The peoples of the northern Great Plains tell many versions of this tale. In some, the children are abandoned for having engaged in minor mischief. In others, the brother is in charge instead of the sister. In another, a wise old woman teaches the girl to perform a ritual that activates the powers of her brother.

But most of the stories end the same way: the two children who escape death make a new life for themselves. They thrive, while the unthinking adults perish.

Once, long ago, some of the People lived together in an encampment. The parents were busy with their activities. The men hunted. The women gathered berries and roots; they made baskets and tanned hides. The children all played together, without adult supervision, sometimes wandering far from the camp.

One day the children traveled farther than usual, so far that they couldn't see the camp in the distance. When they grew hungry, the oldest girl pointed the path out to some of the younger children and sent them back to bring food for them all.

Long before she expected them back, they came running toward her, crying and screaming. "The camp is gone. Our parents have abandoned us," they sobbed.

"It can't be," she replied. "You must have missed the path."

She rounded up all the children, who were getting very hungry now. Together they walked back toward the camp. When they reached the campsite, they found that all that was left were a few fragments of broken tent poles and the dead coals from the fires. Just as the younger children had reported, the adults had all left. The children were on their own.

The older children already knew enough about tracking so that they could have followed the tracks and caught up with them. But their parents had clearly intended to disappear. They had lifted up the ends of their tent poles and the poles of the carrying packs that usually dragged behind the dogs, so that they left no telltale signs. The person bringing up the rear had swept footprints away with brush, so that the children would have no sense at all of which direction they had gone.

Forgetting their hunger, the children spent the remainder of the afternoon fanning out around the abandoned camp. But as hard as they searched, they could find no trace of their parents.

Finally the oldest girl said, "Let's hunt over by the river."

When they reached the water, they waded across, with the oldest children carrying the younger children.

On the far side of the river, one of the girls saw a tent pole lying in the brush. She held it up, and as they walked along the children called, "Mother, Mother, we've found your tent pole."

After a while, they heard a voice calling, "That's my tent pole. Bring it over here."

No child recognized the voice as her own parent, but each imagined it could have been the voice of another child's parent.

They followed the sound. But instead of their parents, they encountered an old woman, who lived all alone. "Thank you for bringing my tent pole back," she said. "Come inside. Let me feed you.

You can sleep here tonight, and tomorrow you can continue searching for your parents. Maybe I can even help you find them. Just be sure, before you fall asleep, to lie down with your heads toward the fire."

The children were so tired that as soon as they finished eating, they lay down with their heads toward the fire and fell asleep.

The children snored and moaned and made all the little sounds people make when they're asleep. Only one girl, who was about eight, was still awake. She had carried her little brother on her back all day, and she was more tired than the others. But she couldn't sleep. She was worried about her little brother, and she didn't trust the old woman.

She lay with one arm over her brother to protect him. She put her head on her other arm in such a way that she could peek at the old woman without being noticed.

When the old woman was sure the children were all sleeping soundly, she put her foot into the fire until it glowed red hot. Then she stepped on the throat of the closest child, burning her instantly to death. Again and again she did this, killing child after child. Even the oldest girl, who was sound asleep, died this way.

As the old woman approached the spot where the girl and her brother lay, the girl leapt up and said, "Grandmother, please allow me to live. You must need someone to help you with your work. I'm very strong, and I work very hard. I'll do anything you ask."

"Very well," said the old woman. "Let's see how you do with your first job. Drag all the bodies of the others out and throw them in the brush for the wild animals to eat."

The girl lifted her sleeping brother and strapped him onto her back.

"Leave him here," the old woman said. "He'll be all right with me."

"I promised my mother I would never let him out of my sight," the girl said.

"Very well, but see that he doesn't slow you down any," the old woman said.

Using all her strength, the girl pulled the bodies of her playmates out one by one and threw them away. It was a horrible task. As numb as she was from all that had happened, it still made her terribly sad to see all of her playmates dead and to know she could not even mourn them properly, or save them from being devoured by wolves.

Each time she felt too weak to continue, she thought of her little brother. Above all, she wanted him to live.

Finally she finished. The woman promised to let her brother and her live until morning. By now the little girl was so tired that she had no choice. Holding her brother tightly, she fell asleep.

Very early the next morning, the old woman shook her awake.

"Go get me some firewood," she ordered.

Again the little girl strapped her brother on her back and set out. She returned with a huge load of cottonwood, taller than her, but the old woman said, "That kind of wood is useless to me. Bring me some real wood."

The little girl went out and brought back an enormous stack of willow branches. But the old woman shouted, "I can't use that wood! Go back and get me some wood I can use!"

The next time the girl returned with birch wood. After that with sagebrush. But each time the old woman screamed that she had brought the wrong wood.

Finally the exhausted child sat on the ground and cried.

After a while a bird spoke to her. "Take her some of the parasites that grow on willow trees," he said. "The ones called ghost ropes. That's what she wants, because she's a ghost."

The girl pulled the parasite plants off the willow branches and brought them to the tent. This time the old woman said, "What a good granddaughter you are. You have brought me wood I can use."

After that, the old woman sent the girl off for some water. First she returned with clear, clean water from the river, but the old woman rejected that. Then she brought back rainwater, even cleaner and purer, which she had harvested from the leaves of plants deep in the forest. But again the old woman sent her away for more.

The girl hunted and hunted until she found a spring of the purest, freshest water, but the old woman rejected even that.

Finally the bird who had helped her before spoke to her again. "You don't understand her yet," the bird said. "The old woman is a ghost. The only kind of water she drinks is muddy and stagnant. Look for water that stinks and is full of worms."

That kind of water was easy to find. The little girl brought some to the old woman, who told her, "At last you are doing well. What a good granddaughter you are."

Then the little brother started crying because he needed to go to the bathroom. "Very well," said the old woman. "Take him out. But hurry back. I have a lot more for you to do."

As the girl left, she let part of her coat catch onto a pole inside the tent. Once outdoors, she removed the coat and staked it to the ground, so that the woman would think she was still close by.

Then she fled, running as fast as she could with her brother strapped to her back.

They came to an enormous river, too wide and too deep for the girl to cross safely with her little brother.

A huge animal with two large horns and thick, heavy fur stood by the water. It was a mountain buffalo, the kind that lives high in the forests.

"If you'll pick the lice out of my head, I'll carry you across," he said.

She did, and he carried the two children across.

Just as they reached the far side, the girl saw the old woman rushing down to the water, waving a huge stick. "Get back here or I'll kill you," she screeched.

But the girl hopped off. Still carrying her little brother, she ran away from the river as fast as she could. The old woman screamed, "No matter where you go, I'll find you! No matter whether you fly into the sky or travel underground, I will always be able to catch you!"

That terrified the girl, but she continued running away as fast as she could, without looking back.

Meanwhile, the buffalo bull returned to the other side of the river, and the old woman demanded, "Take me across right now."

"First you must clean all the sticks from my hair," the buffalo said.

"I don't have time for that. I'm in too much of a hurry," the woman replied, whacking the buffalo hard. "Take me across right now."

The buffalo didn't move.

The old woman started grabbing the sticks and other debris out of the buffalo's hair. But she was in such a rush that she pulled out his hair in great fistfuls, too. Then she started hitting the animal, demanding that he take her across immediately.

Very slowly, the buffalo walked out into the river. "Faster, faster," the woman shouted.

He continued at his own pace.

When he came to the deepest part of the water, he rolled all at once onto his back, so fast that the old woman didn't have time to jump off. She was crushed beneath him, and she drowned. Then, because the animal wasn't just a buffalo, but also a water monster, he ate her, until there was nothing left at all.

The little girl didn't know any of that. She continued to run for days, worried that the old woman would catch them and kill them.

Finally, after many difficult journeys, the children arrived at the new camp of their parents and the parents of the other children.

"Look, we are home, we are back!" the children shouted.

The parents stared at them. "We have no children," they said.

"But mother, this is your son, your little boy," the girl said. "And I am your daughter." Their mother turned her back.

"But father, this is your son, your little boy," the girl said. "And I am your daughter." Their father turned his back.

They went to their uncle and their grandfather, and these rejected them, too.

Finally a man suggested, "Since they can't really be your children, let's tie them up facing each other and hang them in a tree. Then we can leave and go find another camp where we can live in peace."

The little girl and her brother cried and sobbed and begged for mercy. But the people tied them together with rawhide thongs and hung them high in the tree, so that it was impossible to get down.

Their bones would be hanging in the tree to this day, except for the courage of an old man. When he saw what was happening, he thought, "No one will notice me. No one will miss me." So he turned himself into a sick little dog, too puny and weak to be useful to anyone.

People saw the little dog lying there. He had sores all over his mouth, his eyes, and his body. They kicked him and shouted, "Get out of the way." But the little dog ignored them.

After the people had all left, the dog climbed the tree and chewed on the rawhide thongs until the children were free. They cried and cried to think that their parents had left them to die once more. But the little dog just stood there, wagging its tail. When their tears finally stopped, they petted the dog and thanked him. For the first time, the little girl noticed the dog's sores. She found some herbs and rubbed them into the dog, and they started to heal at once.

After a while, a herd of buffalo approached.

"Look at the buffalo, little brother," the girl said, hoping to make him feel better.

When the boy looked at the buffalo, they all fell dead.

The girl was surprised. It was the first time she had known that her brother could help her in any way.

"Look at the dead buffalo, little brother," she said.

The boy looked at the dead animals, and immediately they were all cut up into strips.

"Look at the meat, little brother," she said.

Immediately the meat was all dried.

The girl gave the first and best pieces of meat to the dog.

Then the girl discovered that she too had great powers. She sat on the stack of buffalo skins. Instantly they were all tanned and transformed into buffalo robes. She put the robes together and sat on them again. This time they turned into a tent cover.

She and the dog gathered sticks and bits of wood and old, broken tent poles and put them together into a pile.

"Look at the wood," she said to her brother.

He looked, and the bits of wood came together and formed beautiful new tent poles, strong and straight. She tied them together at the top.

"Look at the tent covering," she said.

He did. The tent and the poles came together and made a beautiful home.

Soon they had everything they needed, including three fine, soft beds. The girl gave the softest and most comfortable bed to the dog.

The girl, the boy, and the little dog lived together happily for some time. The girl made fine clothes of antelope skin for herself and her brother and the dog. They had plenty of food, and a pleasant stream ran past the camp, flowing with pure water. By now, they'd given up all their illusions that their parents loved them or cared for them in any way. But apart from the sadness this knowledge brought, they had a happy life.

Any time they planned to leave the camp, the girl stood outside the tent and shouted, as if she were calling dogs. Each time, four bears appeared out of nowhere and guarded the tent and their other possessions, including the meat supplies.

The three of them might have lived contentedly like this forever, but one day, a man from their old camp discovered where they lived. When he saw their prosperity, he hurried home and said to the others, "Let's move to where the children are. We are starving here, and they have food to spare."

When the people arrived, the four bears kept them from approaching. No matter how much the adults called and pleaded and made promises, the children and the little dog ignored them and wouldn't come out of the tent.

Then the girl said, "My brother, I will go among the people and find a wife for you, one for the dog, and a husband for myself."

So she walked among the people. After inspecting every one, she returned with two beautiful young women and a handsome young man.

She gave one of the women to the dog, and immediately he turned back into an old man. She gave the other young woman to her brother. She herself married the young man. Then she said to her brother, "Now go outside and look at the people."

He did, and they all fell dead. By then, so much had happened that neither the sister nor the brother nor the old man felt any grief at all.

After that, the three couples lived together in the same camp for a long time, helping each other and working together. When children were born to them, they loved them very much, and they did everything they could to give the children a happy life.

THE NEGLECTFUL MOTHER

TOHONO O'ODHAM STORYTELLERS TALK OF A young mother who is so obsessed with playing *toka* (desert hockey) that she abandons her little girl. The girl travels for many days, searching for her mother. When she finds her at last, the mother is so busy playing *toka* that she doesn't even notice when the girl calls her name.

In sorrow, the girl wanders into the desert and disappears into a hole in the ground. Although her mother tries to save her, she arrives too late.

After the daughter vanishes, the mother is so upset that she never plays *toka* again. Where the girl sank into the ground, the first saguaro cactus grows.

In some versions of this story, the girl is a boy. Either way, on a literal level, the story looks at conflicts between a woman's needs as a person and her duties as a mother. On a metaphorical level, it looks at a woman's need to integrate and care for her own inner child.

CONNECTING THE STORY TO YOUR LIFE

1. Until now, most of the narratives we've read have presented old women who are wise, inspiring, powerful, even divine. Here the old woman does have supernatural powers, but she is a symbol for all that is wicked and vile—a stand-in for the people in our lives who appear to be helpful but would destroy us without regret.

Have there been people like that in your own life? If you are free of them now, how did you eliminate them? What is their residual effect on your life today? If you are not free of them, how can you limit their effect on you now?

2. The old woman is also a ghost, a symbol of the people and events who continue to torture us in memories or dreams even after they are gone from our lives.

Who are the people from your past that haunt you, either in waking life or in dreams? How did they hurt you? In what ways do the memories affect you today? In what ways do you still need to heal? If you remember your dreams related to one or more of your ghosts, include them in your journal.

In the story, most of the children don't survive. Looking back, have you known people who have simply been overcome by the forces of evil in their lives? What happened to them? What kept the same thing from happening to you?

3. Go back over this story again, focusing on the parents. Note that, like the old woman, they deliberately hurt their children. In one version of this story, the mother herself hands the girl over to the ghost.

Are there people in your own life who correspond to these cruel parents: parents, siblings, or others whom you thought you could depend on without question, but who let you down in cruel and brutal ways? Or who deliberately set out to hurt you?

Are you still connected to these people? If not, how did you free yourself from them?

If these people are your parents, and you feel you still have more healing to do, read one of the fine handbooks on the topic, such as Susan Forward's *Toxic Parents*.

What parts of the child in you have survived? What parts have died? If you're unsure, ask yourself these questions each night just before you fall asleep for the next week or so. Then pay attention to your dreams. Perhaps some dream images will help you identify these missing parts of yourself.

The parents are also a metaphor for acting in ways that cut us off brutally from ourselves. In your own life, do traces of earlier, destructive behavior patterns remain? If so, what do they relate to? How do you picture yourself breaking free of these patterns?

4. One theory is that people who deliberately hurt others have been badly hurt themselves. At the very least, those who deliberately hurt others tend to be rigid, inflexible, and centered totally on themselves. Thinking of the people in your own life who have hurt you, what do you know about their backgrounds and about the events that may have traumatized them?

In the story, the brutality exhibited by the parents stops in the space of a single generation. When the abandoned children grow up, they make model parents. In real life, wounds, blind spots, and defense mechanisms tend to be passed on from parents to children, through the generations. In your own family, what patterns do you see repeating themselves from generation to generation?

5. Find a place to sit quietly. In your mind, take a trip back to your own childhood. Revisit each of the homes you lived in. Talk to your old playmates. Relive your excitements, your terrors, your pleasures, and troubles.

If you have the inclination and means, plan a real trip back to the scenes of your childhood. Allow yourself time to drift and float and dream as you visit the environments of your childhood and reconnect with yourself as a child. Keep a journal of your journey.

6. In different stories and different traditions, the same animals may represent many different qualities. In the story of Sedna, the bird was a traitor. Here the bird is an ally of the girl, representing intuition, inspiration, understanding, and insight. Similarly, the four bears are powerful allies; they represent courage, strength, and power. Add to your shrine a photo, statue, painting, or other representation of an animal, either domesticated or wild, that you consider to be your own ally.

7. If there are children in your environment, is there one that to you seems particularly to need attention? Plan some outing with that child, something based on the child's interests, not your own. Or spend one hour a week doing some activity with a child that brings the child pleasure and delight.

Chapter Seventeen

The Two Sisters and Their Aunt

A Miwok Tale

Like the previous two stories, this one deals with trust betrayed
by a family member. Once again, children must flee. This time, it
is a wise old man who saves them. In the process the two girls,
like Sedna, become a force of nature.

Once, long ago, in the days when animals and people were still
all alike, there was a beautiful woman who was also a deer.
Her sister-in-law was not nearly so pretty. She was a bear. Everyone
knew the two women by their animal names, Deer and Bear, but
they were people as much as animals. They thought like people and
acted like people. But they thought like animals and acted like animals, too.

From the very first time that Bear's brother brought his wife,
Deer, home, Bear was jealous of her beautiful sister-in-law. Deer
knew this, but she was a gentle, loving woman, and she never believed that her sister-in-law would hurt her.

Time passed, and Deer gave birth to two beautiful little girls.
They were the prettiest children anyone had ever seen, and the happiest. Living in the same house with Deer and her daughters, Bear
grew more jealous than ever. She wanted the little girls all to herself.
She wanted to be their mother.

One day Bear invited Deer to go out picking clover with her. The
girls stayed home by themselves.

For a long time the two women picked clover together, and Bear chatted with Deer as if they had always been best friends.

Finally, in the afternoon, they grew tired and sat down to rest. It was only then, when she sat down, that Deer noticed that her head was itching terribly from lice. Although she could scratch her head, she couldn't get the lice out by herself.

"Let me pick them out for you," Bear offered.

Deer agreed. It was a slow job, and Bear took her time, carefully removing one louse after the other, without pulling her sister-in-law's hair. After a while Deer grew drowsy.

As Deer's head drooped lower and lower, Bear saw her chance. She bit her sister-on-law in the back of her neck, killing her. Then Bear ate Deer.

As the light shifted toward evening, Bear finished devouring her sister-in-law. All that remained was Deer's liver. Bear tucked the liver in the bottom of the basket, then refilled the basket with clover.

When she got home, the two girls came running out to greet Aunt Bear, and that made her happy. Then one girl said, "Where is our mother?"

Bear thought, "They only love her. They don't love me. I've been as good as a mother to them. I deserve better than this."

"You know how slow your mother is," Bear replied. "She'll get home soon. Meanwhile, here's a basket of clover I picked just for you."

She disappeared into a different part of the house.

The girls ate the clover. It tasted delicious. But underneath the clover they found the bloody liver.

"Our aunt has killed our mother," the older told the younger. "If we're not careful, she'll kill us, too."

That night, lying on their beds, the girls whispered a long time, trying to decide what to do.

The next morning, they waited until Aunt Bear had left. Then they gathered their mother's possessions and set out for their grandfather's house. To protect themselves, they left one basket behind.

When Aunt Bear returned, she followed their tracks. But then she heard a whistle, calling from home. Thinking it was them, she hurried back. But it was Deer's last basket, protecting her daughters from Bear.

As the girls traveled, they threw their mother's baskets and tanning tools and other possessions here and there, in all different directions. So when Aunt Bear set out again, she heard the baskets and awls and other items whistling, and she went running off the trail in all directions, thinking she could find the girls.

"I will eat those girls if I find them!" she shouted. "They don't treat me like a mother at all. I deserve better than this."

From every side, she heard whistling sounds, and she didn't know which way to turn.

Finally the girls came to a large river. Daddy Longlegs was walking along its banks.

"What are you doing here?" he asked.

They told him the whole story, and Daddy Longlegs stretched his legs out wide and made a bridge, so they could walk safely across the river.

Soon Aunt Bear reached the river and demanded that Daddy Longlegs help her cross. When she reached the middle of the river, Daddy Longlegs shifted around, so that she fell into the current.

It was moving very fast, and someone else might have drowned. But Bear was a good swimmer, and she reached the far shore.

By now the girls had reached the home of their grandfather, a man who was also a lizard. That is why they called him Grandfather Lizard.

They told him what had happened.

"Where is your aunt now?" he asked.

"Close behind us. She will be here soon."

Grandfather Lizard found two large white rocks and put them in the fire.

When Aunt Bear arrived, she called, "I don't see the entrance to your house."

"It's on the roof," Grandfather Lizard replied. "Through the smokehole."

Aunt Bear climbed onto the roof. "I'm coming down," she said.

"Very well," called Grandfather Lizard. "But I have a wonderful surprise for you. Close your eyes and open your mouth wide."

This made Aunt Bear very excited. She was so eager to eat the girls that she forgot that Lizard was their grandfather and would do anything to protect them.

She opened her mouth, expecting to swallow the girls whole.

Instead, Grandfather Lizard pushed the two fiery stones deep into her throat, and she died a horrible death, scratching and clawing at her neck.

Grandfather Lizard skinned her and cut the skin in two pieces. He gave the larger piece to the older girl and the smaller piece to the younger.

"Here," he said. "Go outside and play."

The girls were so relieved to know their awful aunt was dead, that they forgot all their troubles. They went outside and played, holding the skins on their shoulders as if they were capes, while they ran back and forth.

The capes made a dreadful racket.

Their grandfather smiled. "They're going to be all right," he said. "I know what to do with them. Their racket shows me they're more than just children. They're really Thunders."

At last the girls came inside and told their grandfather they were ready to go home.

"I have a better idea," he said. "You don't belong in that old house. You'll always be grieving for your mother, and thinking about what an evil woman your aunt was. I'll send you up to live in the sky."

The girls took his advice and went to live in the sky. When it stormed, their grandfather could hear them running around. But sometimes they still cried, remembering their mother and the evil deeds of their aunt. That is why, when it thunders, it often rains, too.

LAMENT
A SONG OF THE FOX PEOPLE

 IN "THE TWO SISTERS AND THEIR AUNT,"
human responses, like weeping, are linked
with responses in nature. This is a common theme in Native American traditions. In the following song from the Fox of the Northeast, the singer's weeping and sorrows are linked to the weeping and sorrows of nature.

> *All the spirits weep,*
> *Because I walk weeping.*
> *All the spirits weep,*
> *Because I walk weeping.*
>
> *The clouds will weep.*
> *The sky,*
> *on the day the earth dies,*
> *the clouds will weep.*

CONNECTING THE STORY
TO YOUR LIFE

1. In this story, as in "The Women Warriors" and "The Abandoned Children," two siblings face a terrible and unexpected ordeal together.

If you have a sister, what ordeals have you shared? How has having a sister affected your life? What kind of connection do you have to her today? In what ways are the two of you similar; in what ways different? Is she someone you would select as a sister if you had a choice?

If you have a brother, what ordeals have you faced together? How has having a brother affected your life? What kind of connection do you have to him today? In what ways are the two of you similar; in what ways different? Is he someone you would pick as a brother if you had a choice?

If you have both a brother and a sister, in what ways are your connections to them similar; in what ways different? Looking back to childhood, do you recall ways in which boys in your family were treated differently from girls? If you have children of your own, in what ways do you treat boys differently from girls? Is this a result of your own upbringing, or a result of other life experiences? (Remember the only wrong answer is a dishonest one; the goal is to understand yourself, not to judge yourself.)

Devise a ritual or do some art project in which you honor yourself and your siblings. Or, if you prefer, plan a reunion with your siblings to celebrate and strengthen your bond.

2. Go back through this story another time and look at the connections and interactions going on between Deer, Bear, and the girls. Picture yourself as Deer, so beautiful, innocent, and trusting that she dies. Imagine yourself as Bear, responding to the unexpected changes in her world when a beautiful sister-in-law enters her life. Try to put yourself inside Bear, as her jealousy, anger, and resentment devour her. Finally, picture yourself as the girls, discovering and fleeing a horrifying reality.

At what points in your own life have you been most like Deer? Most like Bear? Most like the sisters? How have you changed since then? How are you still the same?

3. In many of the stories we've read, a woman or girl has had to flee in order to save her life. What literal experiences have you had with fleeing? What triggered your flight?

Are you in flight from something or someone now, either literally or metaphorically? What precipitated your flight? What do you expect the outcome to be?

Creative a mythic narrative about your flight, similar to the stories we've read. Imagine that your story becomes part of your culture's shared wisdom. Sit in your quiet place and visualize a storyteller, long after you are dead, standing by a campfire recounting these tales from your life.

4. Although it seldom seems true at the time, grief is a life-restoring force. This idea is symbolized by the tears of the sisters. They become raindrops, nourishing and healing the earth.

In your own life, what experiences have you had with deep grief? What events, insights, or activities were significant in helping you recover? Did a moment come when you found your grief had become more a part of the past and less a part of the present? Were there times when you allowed yourself to grieve, and times when you didn't? What was going on for you in each case?

Each person has his or her own inner timetable for grief. Some recover quickly. Others require years. If you are grieving now, or if you have grieved in the past, make an illustrated or annotated calendar of your grief to place on your shrine. You may want to draw a wavy line to indicate alternating periods of depression and recovery. Or mark important dates connected to your recovery.

If your grief is mostly past, and occurs infrequently now, what triggers its return? Are you comfortable with the feelings these episodes bring? If not, next time they return, sit quietly and visualize these feelings as entities, spirits, or beings. See if you can befriend them and allow them simply to be.

If you are having difficulty dealing with grief, you may want to join a grief support group, or see a counselor for help in going through the various components of grief successfully (denial, bargaining, depression, anger, acceptance). Or read some of the writings of Elisabeth Kübler-Ross.

5. In some Native American languages, the same word means both mother and maternal aunt. Think of your mother and your aunts. Are there ways in which your aunts have acted like mothers to you?

Put photographs or mementos of these women on your shrine.

Who are the other mother or aunt figures in your life? How did you select them? How are they similar to each other or to your real mother and aunts? In what ways do their personalities reflect some part of you?

If you wish, add photos or mementos of these women to your shrine.

Which of these relationships with blood relatives and substitute relatives have been happiest and most fulfilling for you? Which have been most destructive?

Write a poem about your connection to your mother. Post it somewhere, keep it in your journal, or frame it and leave it on your shrine.

6. Next time it rains, take a long walk in the rain and meditate about the healing power of tears, the healing power of rain. Pay attention to the images that come to mind as you drift along. Use them in a painting, a sand painting, or some other creative project.

Chapter Eighteen

The Woman Who Kept Secrets

A Story from Hopi Country

This story occurs in various forms in the traditions of many Southwest tribes. Among issues it brings up is the question of secrets, particularly secrets between marriage partners. As you read, make a note of any associations and feelings that come up for you.

In some versions of this story, discovering his wife's secrets results in the husband's destruction. In other versions, there is a strong sexual undercurrent: the man sees his wife making love to another man, and the men and women in the kiva are paired up as husband and wife, but not with their spouses from the daytime world.

O nce, long ago, there were four young women who used to grind corn together. They laughed and sang and were happy. Evenings, when the young men had finished working in the fields, they came and stood outside the grinding room. Through the air hole in the wall, they would talk to the young women or tell jokes.

One after another, the young women fell in love and married, until only one young woman remained. She was pretty, and had come from a reasonably happy family, although at her birth her father had been sorry to see that his wife had produced a daughter rather than a son.

After her friends married, the young woman was lonely as she sat in the grinding room singing to herself. But every evening one young man still came around. He was quieter than the others had been, but solid, and he liked the young woman. If she didn't feel like talking, he would stay and keep her company while she ground the corn.

The young woman liked the young man, so she married him. For several years they lived comfortably together, but then she grew restless.

About that time a much more interesting man began coming around to her house during the day, when her husband was out in the fields. "I wish my husband was like this man," she thought. But she didn't tell anyone. She just listened to all his exciting stories and kept them to herself.

One day her husband noticed that the piki bread she sent out into the fields every morning for his lunch tasted old. And yet he knew he'd seen her making piki bread the evening before.

He asked her about it, and she said, "Oh, well, this woman came over who had a lot of company and said she needed some, so I gave her the fresh bread."

But day after day the same thing happened. If she sent piki bread out into the fields with him at all, it tasted old and stale, and each time he asked, she had a different excuse.

For a long time this continued.

The husband was a very kind and gentle man, but eventually he grew suspicious and decided to investigate.

That afternoon, instead of working in the fields, he found a shady place and took a long nap. That night, he only pretended to fall asleep.

After a while, he felt his wife roll over, as if she were moving to the far side of the bed. A little while later, she got up. She bent over very quietly and pulled one of the hairs on his toe, testing to see if he was asleep. He didn't stir.

After that, she walked softly into the other room and brought out a large stack of piki bread. Then she disappeared into the night.

The man dressed and followed his wife. When he saw she was

walking with another man, it made him sick, but he didn't say anything. He just followed.

After a while, his wife and the man she was with disappeared into the side of a hill.

Her husband waited a while, then closely examined the spot where they had disappeared. At first he could find nothing, but then he discovered a secret kiva he had never seen before. Inside, a lot of men and women he knew were holding a secret ceremony, involving a sacred hoop.

He watched as a neighbor woman passed through the hoop, expecting to come out as an animal. But on the other side, she remained a person. Then the leader of the kiva, who was sometimes a man and sometimes a bear, tried to turn back into a bear with the hoop. Again nothing happened.

"Someone must be watching," the bear-man said. He stopped the ceremony, and everyone searched for the intruder. The man had hidden himself so well that for a long time, they couldn't find him.

Finally someone spotted the husband, rolled up in a mat on top of the log roof of the kiva.

Instead of being angry with him, as he'd expected, everyone was nice and invited him inside. His wife made a spot for him to sit with her, and the ceremony continued. Now the hoop worked fine. Some people went through and came out as owls that flew off into the night. Some became foxes, badgers, and other animals.

Finally the man grew sleepy. He rested his head on his wife's lap, and soon fell sound asleep.

When he woke up, he was somewhere he had never been before, on a ledge halfway up a cliff. It was too dark to see, but even so, he could tell the ledge was so narrow that if he moved at all, he would fall to his death. So he lay very still all night.

When morning came, the sun shone so intensely that he grew thirstier and thirstier. "Soon I will die," he said into the silence. But there was nothing he could do.

Finally, a bird flew up and said, "You look thirsty. I'll go get you some water."

When the bird returned, he carried a tiny piñon shell full of water. *That won't be enough,* the man thought, but he was too polite to say so.

He thanked the bird and drank. But instead of a mere sip, the water in the tiny shell lasted until he had drunk all he wanted.

The bird warned him that someone would come and throw corn at him, tempting him to catch it. But if he moved at all, he would fall off the ledge. The bird flew away.

Soon, baked ears of sweet corn started raining down on him. The man was very hungry, but he didn't move at all. Finally the corn stopped falling.

The bird returned and warned the man that the next temptation would be a snake. The bird gave him some medicine to protect himself and told him what to do.

Soon an enormous snake slithered down the cliffside toward the ledge. If the bird hadn't warned the man, he would have been so terrified, he might have jumped off the ledge. Instead, he chewed the medicine, as the bird had instructed, and waited until the snake was very close. Then he spit the medicine hard in the direction of the snake.

Something odd happened. The snake shriveled up, then fell off to one side of the ledge, all the way to the ground.

The man couldn't look down, but it sounded as if the ground must be very far away, because the snake took a long time to fall. Finally, far below, he heard the voices of men and women crying and groaning. Then he understood that there had been people inside the snake, who now lay injured and dying.

When the bird returned, he said, "I have told Spider Old Woman about how your wife put you here on this ledge. She gave me this medicine for you."

The man took the medicine and fell into a deep sleep.

When he woke up, he remembered all at once that he was lying on a ledge. He was terrified to think that he could have fallen off the ledge in his sleep.

But then he heard a voice. It was Spider Old Woman. "You're safe now," she said. He looked around; somehow he had ended up at Spider Old Woman's house. Inside, her house was almost like a kiva.

She set a tiny speck of food in front of him. He was too polite to point out that he was starving to death. He put the speck of food in his mouth, and to his surprise, it grew almost too large for his mouth. He chewed and chewed. The food lasted and lasted. When he was done, he was completely full.

Then Spider Old Woman gave him directions for how to get home. She gave him some medicine and told him what to do about his wife.

The man walked and walked, first to the east, then to the south. By dusk he arrived at his own house.

His wife greeted him happily, as if nothing had happened. She fed him, and they went to bed as always. Neither said a word about the strange experiences the night before.

The man waited until she fell asleep. Then he chewed the medicine Spider Old Woman had given him. He spit the juice into his hand, then rubbed it on her shoulders, first one, then the other, just as Spider Old Woman had told him to do.

Soon his wife got up and, without saying anything, began pacing the room. She walked faster and faster, until she was running like a madwoman all around the room.

Still her husband acted as if he were sleeping.

Faster and faster his wife ran, until suddenly she rushed out the door.

Only then did the man get up. He dressed and followed at a distance.

She was running frantically around.

He blinked his eyes, and when he looked again, she had turned into a white deer.

She ran and ran until she wore out. Then she joined a herd of passing deer.

At that moment, she turned to look at him, and he could see that she was crying.

The man hated what had happened. But he knew Spider Old Woman was right. This woman, his wife, the woman he had loved and thought of as a good woman, had tried to kill him. He couldn't have continued living with her as before.

The man stood in the moonlight and watched the deer as they walked through the night. Then he went back to his home and got on with his life.

THE WEAVER SINGS HER GRIEF

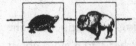 LOVE AND THE LOSS OF LOVE ARE COMMON themes in Native American tales. In this women's song from the Osage of the Great Plains, the narrator grieves for lost love.

> *You have left me behind,*
> *You have left me alone,*
> *You, whose presence made me sing,*
> *You have left me to walk in sadness.*
> *I hurt. I hurt. I hurt.*
>
> *You have left me behind,*
> *You have left me alone,*
> *You, whose presence brought only happiness,*
> *You have gone,*
> *And as I travel, I feel only sadness.*
>
> *You have left me behind,*
> *You have left me alone,*
> *You, whose presence brought only pleasure,*

You have gone,
And as I travel, I feel only grief.

I was content in your presence.
I needed nothing more.
You have left me to walk in sadness.
I hurt. I hurt. I hurt.

THE WOMEN WHO MARRIED THE STARS

SOME CRITICS COMPLAIN THAT CONTEMPORARY women don't take marriage seriously, but this isn't a new situation.

Storytellers among the Salish people of the Northwest Coast tell of five sisters who wished one night that they could have stars for husbands. When they woke up, they found themselves living in the sky with five stars, who were also men. The brightest stars were the oldest, the dimmest stars youngest.

After a while the sisters grew tired of their husbands and of living in the sky. Working in secret, they dug a hole in the sky and made a rope from hazel brush. When the rope was long enough, they slid down it, leaving their husbands behind.

CONNECTING THE STORY TO YOUR LIFE

1. Echoing many other therapists and writers, Clarissa Pinkola Estés says in *Women Who Run with the Wolves,* "The insistence on keeping things private is poison." Do you agree with her, or disagree? Are there situations in which you consider it sensible or justified to keep secrets? What are these situations?

How do you feel about the issue of spouses keeping secrets from each other? Have you been in a situation where you kept secrets from a spouse or other loved one? What factors prompted you to do that? What was the outcome? Have you been in a situation in which a spouse or other loved one kept secrets from you? How did you feel when you discovered the secrets? How do you feel about the situation today?

2. Broaden your look at secrets and their role in your life to include your parents, siblings, children, and friends. Divide your life into ten-year periods and write down any major secrets from each period—both secrets you kept and secrets you suspected or discovered.

Have any of your own secrets remained unrevealed into the present? If so, what feelings do you have when you imagine yourself sharing them with someone? Write about the secrets in your journal. If you are not comfortable revealing them in your journal, give them code names, either plain (Jim, Bob, Doorway) or fanciful (Dagger, Dragon, Lodestone) and record your feelings associated with each secret.

If you have major secrets, consider seeing a therapist to help you work them through. If you suspect other people in your family have major secrets, read John Bradshaw's *Family Secrets* or some similar book.

3. Spider Old Woman has no illusions that the secretive wife will change, and she gives the husband the means to protect himself. In the process, he loses his wife, but gains emotional and physical safety.

What would you lose if your own secrets or your family secrets came out? What would you gain?

As you think about secrets, go outside and find a spiderweb that you can contemplate quietly. What thoughts and feelings come to you during this time? What images or ideas? If you sit long enough and quietly enough, you may receive some sense of direction or clarity related to the secrets. If so, write them in your journal. If not, write about the areas that still seem cloudy or confused.

4. At what points in your life have you felt like the man on the ledge—completely paralyzed and unable to move? What events precipitated these feelings? Who were your allies during this period? How did you, metaphorically speaking, get off the ledge?

5. In this story, large quantities of food come from a seemingly insignificant source. Here particularly, this may be seen as a metaphor for the idea that help comes from improbable places, or for the idea that within ourselves we contain an endless source of spiritual nurturing and emotional sustenance.

In your own life, what techniques have you developed for replenishing these inner emotional resources? When do you feel strong and full of reserves? When do you feel depleted?

6. Part of what makes secrets poison is that they prevent us from being honest about who we are. Picture the process of becoming more honest about who you are as a series of journeys, some short, some long.

In some tribal traditions, it was common to make travel shrines from rocks. When a traveler got up in the morning, she would pick up a stone from the place she had slept and carry it all day. When she arrived at her evening stopping place, she would deposit the stone. Over time, the stones travelers left behind turned into piles, and these turned into shrines, many of which can still be seen on old trails across the Southwest.

If you don't already take regular walks, begin doing so. Imagine each walk as a journey toward healing from secrets. Pick up a stone on each walk and bring it back to your home. At the end of each day's walk, look at the stone you have chosen for the day and go back over whatever topics were most prominent in your mind on the walk. Then add the stone to the pile. As the stones add up, they will serve as memory devices, reminding you of your thoughts, feelings, and moods on previous days.

The stones are a tangible reminder of your journey toward healing and growth. What feelings do you have about your journey and yourself as you observe the pile grow?

Chapter Nineteen

The Quilt of Men's Eyes

A Seneca Tale

On a cultural level, this story includes the tradition, widespread in Native American cultures and tales, that if you are asked to do something four times, on the fourth request, you are obligated to comply.

Thematically, the story might be seen as a reminder of what happens if we agree to do something when our own inner voice is screaming *no*.

Underneath, this is also a story about fear.

In vivid, unforgettable images, it depicts fear of woman's power, particularly the power of the woman who is an artist. The core belief behind this fear is that a woman's artistic power is profoundly destructive.

Once, long ago, when the world was very different from what it is today, two young men who were brothers left their home and parents and went out into the hills to have a good time.

Soon they reached a lodge. Inside, they could hear the sounds of women singing. Instantly, they grew afraid. They were convinced that if they so much as looked at the women, they would die.

"Come on in and sing with us. We're having a lot of fun," the women called. But the young men lowered their eyes and hurried away.

They continued on their way. After a while they came to another lodge. This time they could hear women dancing inside.

"Come on in and join us," the women called. "We'll teach you how to dance."

The young men were terrified. Keeping their eyes down, they hurried away.

As they approached a third lodge, they turned off the path, to stay as far away as possible. Still, they could hear women calling, "Come on in and join us." But they kept their eyes down and hurried away.

Finally they came to a fourth lodge. It was a long lodge, much longer than usual. "Come on in and join us. We have something to show you," the women called.

If the young men could have looked safely inside the lodge, they would have seen a large group of women sewing a blanket, something like a quilt. But instead of sewing on normal decorations, such as feathers, quills, or handmade beads, they sewed on eyes they had torn from the faces of young men. Each time they did that, the men who had lost their eyes wandered blind, hungry, and aimless until they died.

Even though the men were dead, their eyes remained alive, blinking, staring, winking, from their places on the quilt. It was such a frightening sight that no man who looked at the quilt survived.

The young men didn't know any of this. They just knew they were afraid. They didn't want to enter, and would have passed around the lodge on the outside, but because this was the fourth invitation, the young men forced themselves to accept. They went inside, but they looked only at the ground.

"Oh, but you must look at this stunning blanket we are making," the women called to them. "It is the most beautiful blanket anyone has ever owned."

The young men continued to stare at the ground. "Whatever you do, don't look at that blanket," the older brother said to the younger brother. The younger brother assured him he was too terrified to look.

The lodge was so long, it seemed to the young men that whole years passed as they walked from one end to the other, staring at the floor.

At last they came to the fur flap that served as a door. The older brother made it safely out, but just as the younger brother was about to escape, one of the women threw the blanket on the ground in front of him. Before he had time to think, he saw the eyes in the quilt winking and blinking up at him.

Instantly the young man's eyes flew out of their sockets and joined the eyes on the blanket.

Then he was outside. All was darkness. Although he called and called, he could not find his brother.

As he stumbled along, he fell into a spring. Inside the spring he felt himself changing into a duck.

Just then, one of the women making the blanket came down to the spring for water. The duck entered her body.

Soon she gave birth to a baby boy.

The women were delighted. They had never had a baby in their lodge before. They all took turns taking care of the little boy. He became used to a lot of attention and cried at any little thing.

One day it seemed as if nothing any of them did could stop his crying.

At last one of the women said, "Let's give him the blanket to play with. Surely when he sees all those eyes winking and blinking, that will pacify him."

"What if he goes blind?" his mother asked. "What if he dies?"

"Oh, that won't happen," the women replied. "And anyway, we have to do something. He is making too much noise."

The women left the little boy in the lodge, alone with the quilt.

Because his mother was a quilter, the eyes couldn't hurt the boy. But when he saw what the blanket was made of, he folded it into a bundle, put it under his arm, and fled.

When the women discovered the boy was gone, they picked up their hammers and ran after him, planning to bludgeon him to death.

The boy was so much smaller than they were, and so quick on his feet, that every time they tried to hit him, they struck each other instead.

Soon there was only one woman left alive. The boy picked up a fallen hammer and killed her.

With that blow, the spell was broken. He remembered who he was and what had happened and turned back into his old self, the younger brother who had lost his sight. He could see again now, so he set off and hunted until he found his brother. Then the two men removed the eyes from the quilt, a pair at a time. They returned them to the bodies of the dead men, who lay in their graves. That brought the men back to life.

After that, the two brothers went to a cornfield, where they met two beautiful young women. They took the women as wives and had long and happy lives.

THE WOMAN WHO TAUNTED THE WARRIOR

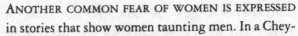 ANOTHER COMMON FEAR OF WOMEN IS EXPRESSED in stories that show women taunting men. In a Cheyenne tale, a young man who is carrying a sacred bow made of boxwood loses courage in the middle of battle. When he returns home, his fiancée makes fun of him by singing a scornful song:

> "You who carried the sacred bow,
> You who carried the sacred bow,
> You should have been carrying a bow made of elm,
> You should have been carrying a bow made of elm."

When he hears the song, the young man is so humiliated that he goes into the hills and sobs.

GIANT-WOMAN

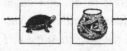

EVEN AMONG PEOPLES WHO HAVE PLACED a high value on the feminine side of nature, there is sometimes a parallel tradition of fear. Stories among the Pueblo peoples of New Mexico include not only the powerful and wise Spider Old Woman, but negative images as well. In a story from the Tiwa-speaking Pueblo of Isleta, Giant-Woman tries to kill the Hero Twins, the children of Mother Moon. And as recently as the early 1900s, Pueblo women were executed for being witches. In 1888 a woman from Sandia Pueblo, accused of being a witch, was killed by an arrow shot into her side.

CONNECTING THE STORY TO YOUR LIFE

1. Because of the widespread fear of women's creativity, many women for generations have dissipated their creative power by stifling themselves. For too many women this becomes a kind of psychic self-mutilation, potentially as damaging in its own way as any other form of self-mutilation. Sometimes women who stifle their creativity begin stifling people around them, too.

Looking back to stories in your family, can you find any evidence of women who were highly artistic or dreamed of having a career as an artist but who stifled that part of themselves? What happened to them? Did their having stifled themselves transmit itself down through the generations and have some effect on you?

In your own life, have there been times when you stifled your creativity or allowed others to do so? What were the short-term consequences? The long-term consequences? Have you regained your creative powers?

List five art projects you would do if you had all the time, money, and talent in the world. Choose the one that means the most to you, or the one that seems easiest to do, and begin working on it in some small, modest way today. For the next two months, work fifteen minutes every day on the project. At the end of two months, make a new plan and a new commitment for continuing with the project until it is done.

2. Fear of women extends much beyond fear of their creativity. What situations in your own family or in other parts of your life have reflected this fear?

Family stories are a powerful tool for transmitting attitudes. What family stories or anecdotes do you recall that reflect some fear of women and women's power? Which family members told those stories? How does their telling of these stories reflect some core personality trait in them?

What family proverbs or admonitions had a similar effect?

Which people in your life—men and women—have acted fearful of women's power in other ways? What has been the effect on you? What steps have you been able to take to restore your sense of wholeness?

At what point in your life did you discover these underlying fears, in others or yourself? Recast these fears as a monster, and create a mythic narrative about yourself discovering, battling, and escaping the monster.

3. What fears do you have today related to your own power or to the power of other women? Write these fears out in sentences that begin, "I'm afraid . . ."

When you have finished the list, write another set of matching sentences that begin, "This fear relates to . . ." and list specific experiences or events.

Write a third list of matching sentences. Begin each one with the words, "I can overcome this fear by . . ."

4. "The Quilt of Men's Eyes" also reflects fear of women working together as a group. In your own life, what empowering experiences have you had when working with groups of women? What experiences have you had with people who were afraid of women in groups?

5. The cruelty of the women in "The Quilt of Men's Eyes" is graphic and unbelievably harsh. Have there been times in your life when you acted in ways that were contemptuous, scornful, brutal, or cruel? What was going on for you? What internal imbalances were you feeling? Are there times when you still feel this way? If so, you may want to seek therapy to help you deal with the underlying wounds that produce these responses in you.

6. If you are married or in a marriage-like relationship, what is your own attitude about balancing your home and family life with other activities you love? What is the attitude of your partner? What compromises have you made gladly? Which ones have you made unwillingly? Make a list of five changes you would most like to see in your relationship, related to this issue. Pick the change that seems least daunting or most important to you and write up a plan for implementing it. What steps do you need to take in the next six weeks? The next six months?

Chapter Twenty

The Kidnapped Wife and the Dream Helper

A Story of the Piegan (Blackfeet)

Because horses play a role in this story, it probably dates back in its present form only to the 1700s. But the core themes, related to the husband and wife's interactions and to the Dream Helper, are probably thousands of years old.

So is a core question the story raises: What is our responsibility to ourselves? When does it take precedence over our responsibility to those we love?

Once a man lived comfortably among his friends and family in a camp along a rushing stream. He was a kind man, and generous, and everyone in the village liked him. After a time, he fell in love with a beautiful woman and married her. Unlike some men, he never wanted to take a second wife. He was always happy with the wife he had.

Time passed, and his wife gave birth to a son. The child grew. One day in late summer, when the boy was old enough to leave behind in the camp, the woman told her husband there was a certain place she wanted to go to pick berries.

"That isn't a good idea," the man said. "Our enemies are always going past that same way this time of year."

But the woman argued and pleaded, and because her husband loved her very much, he finally gave in.

They set out, and some other women followed them because they wanted to pick berries there, too.

When they arrived, the man said to his wife, "You and the other women go down into the ravine where the berries are. I'll go up on the hill and keep a lookout. If I see someone coming, I'll shout, and you must all leap onto your horses and get away."

The women agreed and began gathering berries. They laughed and sang and called to each other as they filled their baskets to the top.

From the hilltop, the man could see all across the countryside. He felt relieved that nothing was stirring. There was not even the dust of animals moving anywhere in sight.

For a while, his attention drifted. He listened to the sounds of the women and felt happy that he had let his wife talk him into coming out here. He felt like a lucky man. It seemed that everything in his life was right.

He scanned the countryside again, and still there was nothing.

All at once he noticed that from a different direction, nearly hidden in a deep ravine, horsemen were galloping toward the women.

The man shouted to the women, then rushed down the hill. Berries and baskets flew everywhere as the women scrambled to their horses. They barely had time to mount before the warriors attacked.

The husband charged back and forth among the women, thwacking their horses to make the animals bolt away. Then he leapt on his own horse and began firing arrow after arrow at the enemy. In order to dodge their arrows and spears, he had to throw himself back and forth constantly, from one side of his horse to the other, using the animal as a shield.

As the enemy gained, he realized he wasn't going to be able to save all the women. So he decided to leave the ones with the slowest horses to the mercy of the enemy and try to help those with the speediest horses get away.

As he charged toward the fastest horses, he heard a voice calling, "My husband, don't leave me."

His own wife's horse was starting to trail behind. "You'll be all right," he called. "You're so beautiful, they won't kill you. I need to help the other women. And I don't want to stay here and die."

"Please don't leave me," she begged. "There is nothing dishonorable about dying together. I would rather be with you and die than stay behind and live."

The man loved his wife very much. He dropped back and allowed his wife to jump from her horse to his own.

That slowed his horse down so much, that the enemy pulled close enough to attack him with war clubs. Once they saw the beauty of his wife, they stopped attacking. They did not want to kill her, and they were afraid they might miss him and club her accidentally.

They grabbed at the woman and tried to pull her off the horse, but she held on to her husband so tightly that although they tore all her clothes off, she remained on the horse.

Cramped in like this, and surrounded by enemies, there was no way the man could protect his wife, ride his horse, and shoot arrows at their enemies. "Let them take you," the man begged her. "We will never get away this way."

"No," she replied. "Let us die together."

He could see that there was no way he could change her mind. "All right," he said. "But you're crowding me so much, I'm all the way up on the neck of the horse. Scoot back some."

She scooted.

"More," he commanded.

She scooted back again.

Then he gave a great shove and pushed her off the back of the horse, into the path of the enemy.

Now that its burden was lightened, his horse charged away. Never once did the man allow himself to look back. He fired arrows on all sides, killing enemies all around, until his horse pulled so far ahead that only two warriors pursued him.

After a long battle, he killed them, too. Then, believing that to go back for his wife was to die, he rode home. All the way he sobbed because he had had to choose between saving his own life and protecting his wife from being kidnapped and raped by the enemy.

Back in the camp, he told the others about the attack. They held a council meeting, and decided to ride out to see if any women had escaped.

When they reached the berry bushes, the bodies of the women lay strewn in the dirt. All had died except his wife, who had vanished with the enemy.

The searchers also found many bodies of the enemy whom the man had killed as he tried to defend the women and save himself. They proclaimed him a great hero.

He didn't feel like a hero. Back home again, he fell into a terrible grief. So did his little boy. For four days and four nights, the father walked around the camp, carrying his son on his back. Night and day they cried. They did not even eat or drink, until the four days of mourning had ended.

Everyone in the camp was very sad about the women who had died. They were sad for the little boy who had lost his mother and the man who had lost his wife.

Finally the man decided he had made a terrible mistake. He decided that no matter what happened, it was better to search for his wife than to sit home mourning her loss. Putting his son on his back once more, he went from lodge to lodge, telling his friends and neighbors goodbye.

The last lodge he reached belonged to a powerful medicine man. Many years earlier, when the man was young, he had seen a vision that set him on the course of his life. In the vision, he saw clearly that he would have great powers, but he would be a solitary man and remain unmarried.

The man had been alone many years, and had never longed for any woman except one. She was very beautiful, very strong, and very clever. Many men had asked her to marry them, and she had turned down every one.

For years the medicine man had watched in silence, as other men tried and failed to make her their wife. Secretly he longed to marry her.

It happened that this woman was the sister of the man who had lost his wife.

When the grieving husband came to his lodge, the medicine man cried with him, thinking how much he would grieve himself if he had lost the only woman he had ever loved.

When their tears finally stopped, the medicine man said, "It is foolish to try to find your wife now. You will die out there, all alone on the hills and mountains and plains, searching for her. Is that what you want for your son?"

"Neither my son nor I can live without my wife," the man replied.

All night the medicine man sat in his lodge and prayed. The next morning, he sent a messenger to the man who had lost his wife.

"You do not need to risk your life looking for your wife. If your sister will promise to become my wife, I will send my spirit helper out to find your wife."

When the sister heard what the medicine man had offered, she laughed. She had no faith at all in the medicine man's power. Without thinking twice, she replied, "I will marry you on one condition. My brother's wife must be home again first, sitting at his side."

Everyone in the village was surprised. They all had great faith in the medicine man. They didn't know the woman was mocking him.

That night, the whole village was awakened by the sound of the medicine man singing. People lay in their lodges and listened. Then they heard a voice that no one had ever heard before.

"Why have you called me forth?" the voice asked. "You know you must never call on me except in time of deepest need."

"That time is now," the medicine man replied. "This man must have his wife back, for his own sake and the sake of his son."

"That is not a good enough reason," the voice argued.

The medicine man's voice softened, and only people in the closest lodges could hear what he replied: "I burn for the woman I love."

After that, even the people living nearest the medicine man could no longer make out the words.

Much later, just as they were falling back to sleep, it sounded as if a great wind came roaring through the camp from the direction of the medicine man's lodge. It was the Dream Helper of the medicine man, hurrying away on his task.

One night soon afterward, the woman who had been kidnapped was lying beside the man who had stolen her and forced her to be his wife. He was sound asleep, but she lay awake grieving, as she had done ever since she arrived, night after night.

At that moment, the Dream Helper found her. He touched her, but she didn't notice, until he gave a shove.

"I am here to take you home," he whispered.

In the dark she couldn't see him clearly. She didn't know who or what he was. But with the faith that comes from complete despair, she got up slowly, quietly, so carefully that the man who now thought of her as his wife heard nothing.

Silently, she followed the figure out of the lodge. Still she could not see him clearly. Without pausing to look back, he walked away from the enemy camp, and she followed without a sound, surprised that no one stirred and no dogs barked.

For a long time they traveled this way, the figure ahead, the woman behind, until the woman grew so tired that she called to the figure and begged him to stop. Without looking back, he stopped, and she sat down.

Each time she got up, he was already up, traveling ahead of her.

They walked this way all night, until she was so exhausted that she lay down and fell immediately asleep.

When she woke up, the figure was there in the distance, just walking away. She rose and followed.

It happened this way for several days. No matter how fast she walked, she could never catch up with the Dream Helper. But no matter how slowly she moved, he never disappeared from sight.

Meanwhile, back in her home village by the creek, the villagers were awakened each night by the sound of the medicine man singing powerful medicine songs. After the singing died, they heard the sound of a sudden wind. Then everything was silent.

At last one evening the woman could go no farther. She stopped and the figure ahead of her stopped but did not turn around. "I have had nothing to eat for days," she called. "And my moccasins are so worn, they are falling off my feet."

The figure did not respond. Exhausted, the woman sank to the ground and fell asleep.

When she woke up, early the next morning, a food pouch she recognized as her husband's and a pair of moccasins she recognized from home lay beside her. She looked all around, but there was no one in sight except the Dream Helper, off in the distance, striding away.

Toward evening of the fourth day, she looked up and saw that for the first time, the Dream Helper had disappeared. In his place a herd of antelope grazed.

When they saw her, the antelope stampeded away.

Silently she walked on in the direction she had been heading. But she was worried. Now that the Dream Helper had vanished, how would she ever find her way home?

The feeling of helplessness grew, and she sobbed harder with each step. It seemed as if the figure she had been following must have been some kind of demon sent to torture her, and that she was about to die forgotten and alone.

She was crying so hard that she didn't hear the sound of a rider approaching from the distance, or smell the dust his horse raised.

When she finally noticed him, he was so close she had no chance to hide. Through her tears she looked at the blurry figure and knew she was going to die.

Then she heard a voice calling, "My wife. It is you. You are safe."

They greeted each other with joy.

Soon it was as if they had never been apart. She climbed on his horse, and together they rode the final stretch back home.

"How did you know to come find me?" she asked.

"The medicine man told me his helper was bringing you," he said.

It was only then that she understood that the figure she had been following was the Dream Helper, sent to guide her home.

When they returned to the village, the villagers came rushing out, exclaiming and shouting because the man had found his wife.

The only person who was upset was the man's sister. She couldn't believe the medicine man had managed to reunite her brother and his wife.

The sister thought about running away. But she knew if she did, she might fall into the hands of their enemies, just as her sister-in-law had. There was no escape. She had to live up to her promise.

She became the medicine man's wife, and he was very happy. Some people say she was happy, too. Others say she was miserable for the rest of her life.

ANOTHER ENDING FOR "THE KIDNAPPED WIFE"

 IN AN ALTERNATE VERSION OF THIS STORY, THE wife has fallen in love with the man who captured her, and when her husband comes to find her, she betrays him. He is caught and tortured, and only the intercession of a kind old woman among the enemy keeps him from dying. Later, the wife's own mother is so angry she wants to kill her. Instead, the wife dies by being pushed back and forth through a fire.

THE DREAMER

 ALL NATIVE AMERICAN TRADITIONS CON-
sider dreams important. In traditional be-
liefs of the Pomo people of California, one woman, known as the
Dreamer, is responsible for the well-being of her people. Through
her dreams, she keeps warriors safe in battle, heals the sick, and
protects children from harm. Through her dreams, people find their
mission in life. She is considered the mother of her people. She is
the center of the circle of life.

CONNECTING THE STORY
TO YOUR LIFE

1. Go back through the story, picturing yourself first as one character, then as another. Which character do you identify most with?
Why? What experiences or situations from your own life come into
your mind as you read? What feelings?

   In particular, how do you feel about the man's having allowed
his wife to be kidnapped rather than staying with her? Was he
saving her, obliquely? Or just saving himself? Are there any situations from your own marriage or long-term relationship in which
it seemed to you that your partner saved himself or herself at
your expense? Were there situations when you saved yourself at
the expense of your partner? Looking back, how do you feel about
these experiences?

2. In this version of the story, the woman forgives her husband
without question. What feelings came up for you, related to this?
What has been the role of forgiveness in your own life? Think

of someone whom you have had to forgive in some major way. Think of someone who has had to forgive you in some major way. Make a poem, song, or narrative related to these instances.

3. In the story the wind symbolizes the great power of the Dream Helper. What does wind represent to you? How do you feel when you stand in the wind? Unless you have unpleasant associations with wind, or unless it is unsafe to do so, take a walk in a strong wind. Or simply stand in a strong wind, with arms outspread and eyes closed, feeling the wind as it passes over your skin.

Write down the feelings, images, and ideas that come up for you during this wind experience. Do a sand painting or other art project that incorporates some of these themes.

4. Again and again in Native American traditions around the country the number four is imbued with special power. Plan a ritual with four components, or a ritual that spreads out over four days. Or do some other activity that honors this ancient tradition: Have lunch with four friends. Write down four important memories from childhood. Place four objects with deep meaning to you at cardinal points on your shrine.

5. Like "The Two Sisters and Their Aunt," this story involves two sisters-in-law. Here, one sister-in-law makes a careless promise. The result: she saves her brother's wife but has to give in to a marriage she doesn't want. In your own life, what experiences have you had with your in-laws? What qualities do you admire in these people; what qualities do you dislike? How has their presence in your family altered family interactions? How has this affected you? Which in-laws do you like best, and why? Which do you like least, and why?

6. If you have not already been doing so, begin paying close attention to your dreams. What themes, images, and feelings recur? Watch for dream allies, or some approximate equivalent of the Dream Helper. Make notes on those dreams, and let yourself free-associate around these dream figures. Are they people from real life or people your psyche has created just for the sake of the dream?

Make a display on your shrine that honors the images and symbols in your dreams. What thoughts, feelings, moods, etc., come up for you as you arrange these items on your shrine, or as you look at them day after day?

Chapter Twenty-one

The Woman Who Built the First Medicine Lodge

A Tale from the Piegan (Blackfeet)

In this powerful love story, a woman has a strong sense of mission and honors it, even when others reject her. Her ability to see clearly what she wants and needs transforms both her life and the life of the man she loves. Ultimately, her wisdom and their deep commitment to one another cause her to bestow a great gift on her people, the institution of the medicine lodge.

Long, long ago, so long ago that people still lived at peace with each other, and no one had ever died in war, there lived a young woman who was very beautiful. Many men wanted to marry her, but she turned them all down.

Her father asked, "Why won't you marry one of these men? You can have anyone you want. Why not pick the one who seems to you to be the most handsome, the richest, and the most courageous?"

"I don't want to," she replied.

Still the young men kept coming. They held contests, and the bravest and fastest came to her afterward and asked her to marry them. But always she said no.

Finally her father said in anger, "The finest men in the whole country have asked you to marry them, and you have said no. You must have a secret lover."

"Oh, this is terrible," her mother said. "Now you will have a baby, and you don't even have a husband. Our whole family will be ruined."

"No," the young woman said. "I am sorry that you don't trust me. But I have no secret lover. It is just that I spoke to the Sun, and the Sun told me, 'Don't marry. You belong to me. I will keep you happy, and you will have a long and healthy life.' "

"Very well," said her father. "You must do as the Sun says." After that neither her mother nor her father pressed her to get married.

Among the people there was a young man who was very poor. Although he was strong and brave, his face was puckered with a terrible scar. His father and mother and all his relatives had died, and he was homeless. People felt sorry for him, and they let him stay a day in one lodge, a day in another, but he had no lodge of his own, and no mother or sister or wife or grandmother to tan a robe for him or sew a pair of moccasins for him. His only possession was an ancient robe, full of holes.

The other young men of the village liked to make fun of him. One day they told him, "Hey, look, that beautiful woman won't marry us. But maybe she will marry you. You are the most handsome and the richest of us all."

The young man knew they were making fun of him. But he decided to try anyway. *After all, she has turned everyone else down,* he thought. *What difference does it make if she turns me down, too?*

He went to the river and waited until the young woman came to get water for her family.

"May I speak to you?" he asked. "I would like to stand in the full light of the Sun and talk to you openly for everyone to see."

The young woman was pleased at the way he spoke, and she agreed.

"I have watched you a long time," the young man said. "I have seen how you refuse every man who asks. I am poor, so poor I have no food, no lodge, no clothes, and no relations. And I have this scar on my face. But it is my face that is scarred, not my heart. The other young men have made fun of me. They have said I should ask you to marry me. And I have decided they are right. I have nothing to offer you but myself, but I would like you to be my wife."

The young woman covered her face with her robe and moved the toe of her moccasin around in the dirt. For a long time she thought about what he said. Then she spoke. "It is true that I have turned down all the richest young men and the handsomest, and those that have the most courage. But maybe you are right. Maybe I should marry you. My mother will build us a lodge. My father will give us dogs. My family will give us robes and furs and clothes. We will have everything we need. Yes, I will marry you."

The young man was so surprised and so pleased, he reached out to hug her and give her a kiss.

"No. Not yet," she said. "There is just one thing. The reason I have not married until now is that I have spoken with the Sun, and he says that I belong to him. If you want me as a wife, you will have to visit the Sun. You will have to get his permission."

"How can I possibly do that?" the young man asked. "No one knows where the Sun lives. No one has ever traveled all that way before."

"You must have courage," the woman said. "And when you reach the lodge of the Sun, you must ask him for some sign, so that I will know you have spoken to him."

The young man was very sad. He sat on the ground and covered his face with the tattered old robe and felt sorry for himself.

Finally he remembered an old woman who had been very kind to him. He went to visit her and said, "Please forgive me for asking this, but I am very poor, and I have no moccasins. I must go on a long journey, farther than anyone has ever traveled before. Please take pity on me, and make me a pair of moccasins."

"But why would you travel so far?" the old woman asked. "There is no war. There is no reason to travel."

"I cannot tell you where I am going," the young man said. "But I am in trouble, and I must leave."

The old woman had a kind heart, and she was very wise. She asked no more questions. She made him seven pairs of fine moccasins, with thick soles and fine blue beads. She filled a sack with pemmican made from meat, fat, and berries. Then she gave him a blessing, and he left.

When he reached the top of the bluffs that overlooked the place where his people had their camp, the young man stood a long time staring down on the lodge of his people and the lodge of the woman he wanted for his wife. He felt a great sadness. "I want her to be my wife," he said to himself, "but I may never see her again. I may never see anyone I know again."

Feeling terribly sad and alone, he began his journey.

For many days he walked, across prairies, along rivers, in the woods, and over mountains. As much as he could, he ate food that he found along the way: berries, roots, small animals. But still his food sack grew lighter, and he worried that he might starve before ever finding the lodge of the Sun.

One day he came to the home of a wolf. "Greetings, brother," the animal said. "What are you doing so far from home?"

"I am searching for the home of the Sun. I need to speak to him."

"I have traveled very far," the wolf replied. "I have crossed prairies and passed through valleys and climbed mountains, but I have never reached the home of the Sun. I do not know where he lives. Perhaps Bear knows. He is very wise."

The man traveled some more, until he reached the lodge of the bear.

"Brother, why are you traveling all alone?" the bear asked. "Where is your home?"

The young man felt safe with the bear. He explained his mission.

"I am sorry," the bear replied. "I know all the mountains and rivers for many miles around, but I have never reached the lodge of the Sun. Go ask the badger. He knows a lot that even I don't know."

Badger received the man warmly, but he also did not know the home of the Sun.

Finally, just as his food ran out, the man reached the home of the wolverine. "I'm sorry to bother you," the man said, "but everything has gone wrong. I have no more food, and even if I did, I do not believe it would be possible to find the home of the Sun."

"Of course it is possible," the wolverine replied. "I know where the Sun has built his lodge. He lives on the far side of the Big Water. Tomorrow I will show you the trail."

When the young man reached the edge of the Big Water, and saw how far it stretched, his heart was very sad. He was hungry, and the soles of the last pair of moccasins had worn all the way through. He was so far from home, he felt he could never return. Yet he knew that there was no way he could go on, to the other side of the Big Water.

He sat in the sand by the sea and began composing his death song. And as he did so, he thought of the woman he had left behind. At first, when he had asked her to marry him, it had been almost a game. But in the days and weeks of traveling, he had grown to love her very much.

Now it all seemed useless. He would die alone. And the woman he loved would spend her whole life belonging only to the Sun.

For a long time he thought these thoughts. When he finally opened his eyes, he saw two large, beautiful swans swimming toward him.

"What are you doing here?" they asked. "Why are you so far from home?"

"It seems I have come here to die," the young man said. "I just wanted to marry the woman I love." Once again he told his story. "But I have no way to cross the Big Water," he said. "Now I am going to die."

The swans felt sorry for him. They took turns carrying him on their backs until they reached the other side of the Big Water.

There the man found a trail. Off to one side lay a bundle. The man opened it and found the most beautiful bow and arrows he had ever seen, the most finely painted shield, and the most beautifully woven shirt. He closed the bundle back up and left it lying where he found it.

A little farther down the road, he met a handsome young man with long hair and exquisite moccasins made of colored feathers.

"My weapons were lying beside the trail," the man said. "Did you see them?"

"Yes," the traveler replied.

"But you didn't take them?"

"They didn't belong to me."

"I see that you are not a thief," the man said. "What is your name? And why are you here?"

"I am called Scarface, and I am going to visit the Sun."

"I am Dawn Star," the man said. "My father is the Sun. Come visit our lodge, and wait for him to return tonight."

Scarface had never seen such a fine lodge before. The outside was covered with beautiful paintings of remarkable animals that he had never heard of. They were the medicine animals of the Sun. Behind the lodge hung remarkable weapons, completely unknown to his people, and the most beautiful clothes he had ever seen. All belonged to the Sun.

Inside the lodge sat the Moon. She was the wife of the Sun, the mother of Dawn Star. She gave Scarface something to eat and asked him why he had come.

Scarface told her his story. "I have come to ask the Sun if I may marry this woman who says she belongs to him."

That night, the Moon hid Scarface under some robes. When the Sun returned home, he said, "Someone is here. I can smell it."

Scarface came out from under the robes, and Dawn Star presented him to the Sun. "I know he is a good man, father," said Dawn Star. "I have seen it in his actions."

The Sun invited Scarface to stay in his lodge and be a companion to Dawn Star.

Scarface agreed.

The next morning when he woke up, the Sun was already gone. The Moon gave the two young men a pouch of food and told Scarface, "You may go anywhere you wish, except the Big Water. Never hunt there, or let my son go there, because enormous birds live there. They have sharp beaks and powerful claws, and they have killed many people, including all my other children. Only Dawn Star survives."

Scarface agreed to avoid the Big Water.

For a long time, Scarface stayed with the Sun, the Moon, and Dawn Star. He wanted to talk to the Sun about the real reason for his long journey, but the Sun is very powerful, and Scarface knew he would have to wait for the right moment.

One day, Dawn Star asked Scarface to go with him to the Big Water to kill the giant birds.

"We mustn't," Scarface said. "Those birds would kill us. They have killed all your brothers and sisters. Your mother asked me never to let you go there."

Dawn Star insisted. Without waiting for Scarface, he ran toward the water.

Scarface called and called, but Dawn Star ignored him. In the distance Scarface could see the giant birds flying toward him, with talons outstretched.

Scarface ran after Dawn Star, faster and faster, until he was running ahead of his friend, so that the birds would attack him first. One by one he fought them off, killing them with his spear, until none remained.

The young men cut off the birds' heads and took them home.

When the Moon learned that Scarface had saved her son's life, she wept.

That night, she told the Sun what Scarface had done. "Now you too are my son," the Sun said. "Tell me what I can do for you."

Only then did Scarface tell the Sun his story. He started at the beginning, and told it straight to the end. "The woman I love has said that you have told her not to marry," he concluded. "I have come here to ask you to release her and let her marry me."

The Sun spoke. "I made the earth, and everything that exists. I made the mountains and the forests. I made the rivers and the prairies. I made the animals and the people. I made you and the woman you love."

"Then let her marry me," Scarface said.

"The woman you love is a very good woman," the Sun said. "She was wise to turn away all those men, because they didn't really love her. She was wise to listen to me. Now I give her to you. She will be your wife. She will have a long life, and so will you."

The Sun took Scarface outside and showed him the whole world. "The raven is the smartest animal," the Sun told him. "And the buffalo is the most sacred. The buffalo belongs to me, but I have given him to people, for food, for shelter, for clothing."

The Sun told Scarface, "The most sacred part of your body is your tongue. It has the power of the Sun. It belongs to me."

The Sun continued, "Here is what you must tell the woman who is to be your wife When a man falls ill, or encounters danger, and he recovers, his wife must build a medicine lodge in my honor."

He explained all the details of how to construct a medicine lodge. When the Sun had finished, he rubbed herbs on the young man's face, and the scar disappeared. Then the Sun handed him two raven feathers and said, "This is the sign the woman you love asked for. The husband of the woman who builds a medicine lodge must always wear two raven feathers, just like these."

When the Sun finished speaking, the Sun, the Moon, and Dawn Star gave the young man many presents. Then the Sun showed him a shortcut: the Milky Way. The young man followed that trail, and very quickly he reached home.

He arrived at dawn on a hot day. Wrapped in a buffalo robe, he sat on the edge of the bluffs near the village and looked down on his people going about their daily life. Because of the heat, people had lifted the lodge skins onto poles so that they would have shade, and a breeze could blow through the lodge. They passed the day sitting in the shade and visiting with their chief.

It was the chief who noticed the young man first: a solitary figure, sitting on the bluff, covered with a buffalo robe. All day the chief watched, and noticed that in spite of the heat, the figure kept the robe wrapped tightly around him, from head to toe, so that the only part of him that showed were the two raven feathers sticking out of his hair.

As the day ended, and darkness approached, the chief asked the young men: "Who is that person sitting so still over there? It is the hottest day of the whole summer, but still he has kept his buffalo robe wrapped tightly around him. He has not eaten or drunk all day. He must be a stranger. Please invite him to join us in a feast."

The young men of the village approached the figure on the hill and said, "Welcome, stranger. Our chief wants to know why you have stayed out here all day in this heat. Come with us to the shade of our lodges. Come and feast with us."

Then the young man threw off the robe. The young men of the village were astonished to see this stranger wearing such beautiful clothes, and carrying weapons they had never seen. Then they looked at his face, and even without his scar they recognized their old friend.

"What happened to you? How did you get so rich? Who took away your scar?" they asked.

They ran ahead and shouted to the villagers that Scarface had come home.

People gathered around to greet him, but the young man said nothing to anyone until he approached the young woman he loved.

From his head he took the two raven feathers and handed them to her. "The way was long and hard," he said. "But the Sun listened to me. He said I may take you as my wife. He sent you these."

Then the woman knew that no one had ever loved her so much. With happiness and joy, she married the young man. In honor of the danger he had passed through, she built the first medicine lodge.

The Sun smiled on them and gave the two a long and happy life. When they were very old, their great-grandchildren came one morning and said, "Wake up. It is time to eat." But the two did not stir. Their shadows had gone away, to the place of the dead, in the Sand Hills.

PRAYER TO THE SUN

 REVERENCE FOR THE SUN IS COMMON IN
Native American traditions across the con-
tinent. This Piegan (Blackfeet) prayer from the northern Great Plains
reflects the close connection Native peoples feel toward the sun.

> O great Sun in the sky
> Look down on me in pity.
> Look down on me in kindness.
> Long life. Long life.
> I pray for your long life.
> I will help you reach old age.
> I will call on all your children
> To help you reach old age:
> Evening Star, Morning Star,
> The Seven Stars, the Clustered Stars.
> These stars and all your other children,
> I can call on them for help.
>
> Look kindly on me, O Sun,
> May I, like you, live a good life.
> Look kindly on me, O Sun,
> That I may watch my children reach old age.
> Look kindly on me, O Sun,
> Guide me, support me, have pity on me,
> That I may lead a long and peaceful life.

CONNECTING THE STORY TO YOUR LIFE

1. As this story opens, the young woman is fighting society's expectations. Everyone expects her to marry, including her parents. When she doesn't, they imagine the worst.

What feelings, memories, and associations does this part of the story bring up for you? At what points have you had to fight for your right to lead your life the way that seemed best to you? At what points have your parents or other people close to you imagined the worst when you didn't do as they expected you to do? What did you do to set their minds at ease, or to ensure that you would be free to be who you needed to be?

2. When the young man expects to die, he composes a death song: a final statement in life as he makes his transition to the other world. At what stage are you in the journey toward accepting the inevitability of your own death?

If you feel comfortable doing so, compose a short death song, based on who you are now and what your life has been like. If you are so inclined, sing the song into a tape recorder, write it down, or sing it to a friend.

Imagine that you will die within the next twenty-four hours. Your affairs are in order. You have told those you love goodbye. You have made your peace with death. Enough time remains for you to sit and write a letter of advice to someone who is exactly like you yourself are at this moment. What advice would you give? Write the letter, summarizing the advice of the dying you to the present-day you.

What changes do you need to make in your life, based on that advice? If you are so inclined, draw up plans for making those changes: a six-week plan, a six-month plan, a one-year plan. Post them prominently somewhere, or put them with your journal and other important papers.

3. What does the young woman's promise to the Sun represent to you? What kinds of promises or commitments to yourself have you made that could be seen as similar to this young woman's promise? What were the circumstances that led up to your vow? What was the result of that vow? If you were unable to keep your promise to yourself, how did you feel? How do you feel about the whole experience now, looking back?

4. The young man's journey represents an abbreviated version of the classic mythic quest: he leaves home, young, innocent, full of fear and hope. After many adventures, difficulties, and maturing experiences, he is a new person. He returns home, where he becomes a force of transformation among the people who once considered him an outcast.

What, in your life, has been your own version of that quest? Where are you on your journey now? Who were the allies, like the wolverine and the swans, who appeared when you most needed them? Who were the attack birds, who could easily have killed you?

If you feel that you are floundering on your quest, or have lost your way, read one of the manuals on these journeys of the soul, such as *The Heroine's Journey* by Maureen Murdock.

5. In Piegan (Blackfeet) tradition the medicine lodge was a powerful place of safety and of transformation, where physical and spiritual wounds could be healed that were otherwise unhealable in ordinary life.

If you could build your own medicine lodge, what would it look like? What objects would you place inside it? When would you use it?

Looking back, at what points in your life would you have found a medicine lodge particularly meaningful or useful? Sit quietly with closed eyes and go back over those periods, imagining yourself sitting inside the medicine lodge, undergoing healing rituals.

6. Pictures of powerful medicine animals decorated the lodge of the Sun. Make a drawing or a display on your shrine of those objects from your own life that have had the most power to calm you, soothe you, center you, or help you feel most fully yourself.

Imagine yourself as a mural painter. Close your eyes and picture yourself creating a vast mural that includes these objects, along with your own personal medicine lodge, and healing scenes from your life.

Chapter Twenty-two

The Dream of Double Woman

A Lakota (Sioux) Tale

Like "The Quilt of Men's Eyes," this story explores woman's creativity, but in a completely different way. Here, there are only two dangers: If someone tries to stop the quill worker's creativity, she or he may come to harm. And if the mythic first quill worker ever completely finishes her work, the world as we know it will end.

Long, long ago, there lived the most beautiful woman of all. She had long, thick blue-black hair, and everything about her was more perfect than it had ever been in another woman or would ever be again. Although she was human, she was also a deer. That is one reason why she is called Double Woman.

Once a young man wanted to marry her. He didn't know she was a deer-woman. He thought she was an ordinary woman. For a long time, she said no, but he kept persisting. Finally, she agreed. But when he embraced her, she turned into a doe and bolted away.

Angrily the man called to his friends, and they set out to hunt her. For days they chased the doe through the hills, until finally they cornered her. Without considering that this was the woman he claimed to love, the man and his friends rushed forward and killed her.

Immediately the young man lost his ability to speak. He snorted and pawed the ground with his feet, like a deer. Soon after that, he died.

Since then, men have known never to approach a woman who is alone on the plains or in the forest, because although she looks like a normal woman, she may actually be the deer-woman, Double Woman. Any man who touches her will die. And anyone who dreams of Double Woman will find his life changed forever.

These events all happened so long ago that at that time it had never occurred to anyone that porcupine quills might be useful for something. When a porcupine was killed, the quills were thrown away.

One day, though, a beautiful young woman fell into a deeper sleep than she had ever experienced before. In her dream, Double Woman came to her. She looked more beautiful than ever, with spots of bright red paint decorating her cheeks. She was wearing a fine buckskin dress covered with the most intricate quillwork imaginable.

The young woman had never seen quillwork before, even in a dream. She reached out to touch the dress, and Double Woman said, "I have chosen you to learn this sacred art."

Double Woman took the young woman into the brush and showed her how to find plants that produced fine dyes, one each for the four directions: yellow, blue, red, and black. After that, Double Woman brought the young woman into the most beautiful lodge she had ever seen. It was a finely wrought teepee, a medicine lodge, with twenty-four poles. Inside the lodge lay a porcupine, a large white bird, and a buffalo hide.

Then Double Woman showed the young woman how to split the quills of birds and dye them. She showed her how to pull the quills from the porcupine without hurting herself, and how to arrange them by length.

For four days and four nights Double Woman and the young woman worked together, attaching the quills to the buffalo robe. It was the most beautiful robe the young woman had ever seen.

When the young woman woke up, she told the elders all that had happened in the dream. They ordered a special lodge to be built for her, and sent the young men to bring her a porcupine, a large white bird, and a tanned buffalo hide. The young woman herself went into the brush and found the plants she had seen in her dream. Then she retreated into her new lodge, coming out only to sleep and eat.

Finally one day she emerged carrying a quilled buffalo robe almost as beautiful as the one in her dream. She showed it to the other women and taught them what to do, and from that day on, women have practiced the sacred art of quillwork. Even today, when a woman needs guidance in her art, Double Woman will appear to her in a dream.

If a man tries to stop a woman from performing this sacred art, Double Woman will appear to him. If he tries to make love to Double Woman, he might, like the young man so long ago, turn into a deer and die.

It is said to this day that sometimes you can glimpse the woman who dreamed of Double Woman and introduced quillwork to the people. She sits in the moonlight, sewing away. Or maybe you'll glimpse her inside a cave.

She is old now, and she has flattened so many porcupine quills with her teeth that nothing remains but stubs. Her dog sits beside her, watching everything she does. A pot of herbs cooks on the fire. Sometimes she puts her work down to tend the fire or stir the herbs. When she does, her dog unravels her work. And it's a good thing, because if the woman who sits doing quillwork in the moonlight or in her cave ever finishes her work, at that very moment the world will end.

QUILL SOCIETY

AS A RESULT OF THE YOUNG WOMAN'S DREAM OF Double Woman, a new women's organization, the Quill Society, was formed. As the generations passed, rules and customs evolved. Only skilled quill workers could join. When it was time for a meeting, the hostess would send out one of the oldest members of the group to invite guests. Each quill worker brought samples of her work, and a great feast was held.

Because the society was founded as a result of the first quill worker's dream, it was considered *wakan* (sacred).

WHEN DOUBLE WOMAN APPEARS

ACCORDING TO LAKOTA TRADITION, WHEN DOUble Woman appears to a woman in a dream, she will often invite the woman to enter her lodge. Inside, at the back, sit two women. They invite her to choose which side of the room to enter. Along one wall hang tools, such as those used for dressing animal skins or making carrying bags and other items from rawhide.

Along the other wall hang beautiful bags made of rawhide.

If the dreamer chooses the side of the room which contains the tools, it means she will lead a happy, productive, conventional life and grow very prosperous. If she chooses the other wall, it means she will focus her life energy on seducing men.

At the end of the dream, the women turn into black-tailed deer and run away.

After a dream of Double Woman, the dreamer invites others who have dreamed of Double Woman to a feast in her honor.

CONNECTING THE STORY
TO YOUR LIFE

1. In this story, as in a number of others, colors have some special meaning, in this case yellow, red, blue, and black. Using crayons, paints, colored papers, colored sands, colored fabrics, marking pencils, or some other medium of your choice, experiment with colors and color combinations. Which ones soothe your eye or appeal to you most?

Create a collage, abstract painting, sand painting, or other artwork using these colors. Place it where it will be the last thing you see before you fall asleep and the first thing after you wake up. What dreams, associations, feelings, moods, etc., come up for you when you look at these colors? Write about them in your journal, or talk about them into a tape recorder.

2. This story ends with the poetic idea that if the quill worker ever completely finishes her work, the world will end. What associations or images come up for you, related to this? Playing with this theme, come up with your own story of how the world will end.

3. Read the story again, focusing on Double Woman in the prelude. Someone who claims to love her tries to kill her when she turns out to be a different creature from what he thought she was.

What experiences from your own life does this story remind you of? Create a narrative focusing on these experiences. Or create some chant that will help you finish healing from them.

What does Double Woman represent to you? Why? Write a few paragraphs about her in your journal.

If you can, buy some quillwork or other craft work by a Native American woman and put it on your shrine. Or go to a museum that contains such items, or check out a book with photographs of them, and find a piece that particularly catches your eye.

Study the piece until you have it more or less memorized and can see it in your mind. Then sit quietly and meditate about all the Native American women who have come before you on this continent.

Imagine yourself as an ancient quill worker. What would your life have been like? Watch that woman in your mind. Ask her if she has any advice for you. If so, thank her, then write the advice down and give it a place of honor on your shrine, on a wall, or in your journal.

4. This story is partly about the sacred origin of art. Think of the art forms or particular art pieces that you find most meaningful. What about them is sacred to you? What inner facet of you do they resonate with?

The story also contains the idea that it is from a woman of great beauty and power—an idealized internal woman—that sacred arts emerge.

What internalized images do you have of an ideal woman, a sacred woman, or a wise woman? At what times do you feel most in touch with this wise woman? Least in touch? What insights have you had about the wise woman inside you since the last exercises you did related to her?

Do you have a sense of there being some sacred art within you? If you don't know, look to your dreams, or to the wise woman inside you for an answer.

5. In some versions of this story, the young woman who dreams of Double Woman reaps some of Double Woman's power: She can simply lay the quills down, cover them with buckskin, sing a sacred song, and when she is finished, the quillwork will be done.

This image provides a useful metaphor for certain stages of the artistic process: For the artist, when the work is going well, time stops, and it seems as if the work creates itself.

What experiences have you had with this phenomenon in your own life? What were you doing when you felt that way? What can you do to arrange your life or your work to increase the frequency of such experiences?

Chapter Twenty-three

The Woman Who Married the Sea

A Samish (Coast Salish) Tale

The peoples of the Northwest Coast tell many versions of this story. In one, from the Coos people of southern Oregon, the woman sends the People two whales each year as a sign of her affection.

On a literal level, the story reminds us of human dependence on and connection with the sea. On a metaphorical level, it shows the importance of the unconscious and the importance of giving the psyche what it needs.

Once, long ago, the People lived near a channel in the sea. The sea was good to them, and they found more than enough to eat: clams, salmon, crabs, mussels.

One day, a young woman walked along the shore, picking up crabs and digging up clams and other food to take home to her family. She had almost enough collected for her family to eat in a day. But then one of the clams slipped out of her hands and fell into the water. She walked in and picked the clam up, but it fell out of her hands again, farther out in the water.

This happened several times, until she was up to her waist in the sea.

She was ready to turn around and go back home without the clam when she felt a hand inside the water grab her hand. She tried to shake it off, but the hand held on tight.

Before she could scream for help, she heard a voice talking softly to her, from somewhere inside the water. "You are the most beautiful woman who has ever lived," the voice said. "I am so glad you have come to visit me."

Then the hand let go, and the young woman hurried home to her family.

The next day the same thing happened. This time, the hand held on to her a little longer, and the gentle voice told her about life in the bottom of the sea and how beautiful the world below the sea was.

For four days in a row this happened. On the fourth day, the voice said, "I love you very much. I want you to come and live with me in this wonderful world at the bottom of the sea."

Then a handsome young man came out of the waves. He was the sea itself, taking the form of a man. The young woman brought him home with her, and he asked her father to let her marry him.

The young woman was willing, but her father refused. "I don't care how much you love her," he told the young man. "I can't let my daughter go live in the sea."

The man from the sea grew angry. "If you won't let her come with me, I will take away all your food, and the people will starve." But still the father of the young woman said no.

The man from the sea returned to his home, and from that day, no matter how far out the young men went in their canoes, the salmon grew scarcer and scarcer. No matter how carefully the young women searched the beaches, they could not find the clams and crabs and mussels that they had formerly brought home.

Soon people were starving, and they moved inland to catch fish from the freshwater streams, but the streams dried up, and once again people grew hungry.

The young woman saw all that was happening, and was sad.

One day, without waiting for her father's permission, she left the camp by the freshwater stream and walked all the way to the sea.

She stepped into the water, but nothing happened. "Listen to me," she called softly. "My people are starving. There is not even any water to drink. Soon we will all die. Please give us back our food."

The young man rose from the waters again. "I love you," he said. "I want you to be my wife. If you will marry me, I will provide food for the people once more."

The young woman felt sad. She knew her father well. She was sure he would not give in.

Each day she returned to the sea and pleaded for her people. Each day the man in the sea replied the same way. Each day her father said no.

Finally on the fourth day, she told her father, "If you do not give me to the sea, all the people will die. It is beautiful in the sea. I will have a happy life. Give me to the sea. Let our people live."

Then the father saw that what his daughter said was true.

Once more he received the young man from the sea in his home. "You may marry my daughter on two conditions," he said. "You must promise to keep her happy. And you must let her return to her family one day each year."

The young man agreed, and the young couple were married at once.

Those who had enough strength walked down to the beach and watched the young woman disappear into the water with her new husband, just as the sun was setting.

The last her family and friends saw of her was her long black hair as it drifted on the surface of the sunset-painted waters. Then even her hair disappeared.

The very next day, the salmon returned. Crabs scuttled across the beach, and once again the watery air holes that revealed the presence of clams popped out along the shore.

No one was ever hungry again.

As the end of the first year approached, food grew even more plentiful. There was so much salmon and so many crabs, mussels, and clams, there was no way the people could eat everything.

Then the young woman returned for a visit. She was more beautiful than ever, and it was easy to see how happy she was.

The next year, the same thing happened, and the next. By the fourth year, though, it was clear to everyone on the shore that it was very hard on the woman to come back to her old home. On dry land, she could scarcely breathe anymore. Barnacles grew on her cheeks. Wherever she walked, a cold wind blew.

The people gathered in a council and said, "It is clear that you love your new life. You have given us back our life. We have everything we need. You don't need to return again. We set you free from your promise."

After that, the young woman stayed in her home in the sea. But she continued to guard her people, and her spirit returned many times.

Sometimes when the light was right, people would go down to the narrow channel in the water and see her dark hair floating on the surface. When young men went to sea in their canoes, they thought of her, and she made their passage safe. And in every generation, mothers told their children the story of Our Mother, the woman who gave us life, the woman who married the sea.

THE WOMAN WHO GAVE BIRTH TO THE WIND

 STORIES FROM MANY TRADITIONS link women to the elements. In a Chippewa tale, a woman has a premonition that something bad will happen to her daughter, so she warns her never to face east when she squats in the woods to urinate.

One day the young woman forgets. Immediately, a whirlwind swirls around her, stripping off her clothes and impregnating her.

During her pregnancy, four babies battle violently inside her, causing her great pain. At the moment of birth, they fight more than ever, each trying to be the first to emerge. They struggle so violently that it blows their mother into tiny pieces, scattered far and wide. The quarrelsome children separate, one going north, one south, one east, and one west. As they grow up, they take on their true identity, as the Four Winds.

CONNECTING THE STORY TO YOUR LIFE

1. If you live near the ocean, take time, if you can, to go to the beach on a quiet day and sit watching the water. If that isn't practical, sit quietly and visualize yourself at the seashore. Watch the waves rolling in, one after another, cresting white as they ride into the shore. Hear the sound of the pebbles at the shoreline, washing back and forth. Taste the salt in the air. Smell the breeze.

Let your mind float. What images come to you as the waves ride in? What memories? What feelings?

Write these in your journal, or use them to create a poem, narrative, or song.

2. In the story, a whole nation suffers terribly because of the conflict between the man from the sea and the woman's father. What conflicts have occurred between men in your family? How have they affected you? How were they resolved? Imagine yourself as an ancient singer, chanting to heal the wounds within you and within the men in your life.

Because the man from the sea is angry, he deprives people of something essential: food. What were the patterns related to anger in your own family? Looking back, do you see these patterns as healthy or unhealthy? Why? What have been your experiences with people outside your family getting angry at you? In what ways have you suffered? In what ways have you learned to protect yourself?

Think of your own anger. What situations trigger anger in you? For some people, anger points to their areas of denial. Treat your anger as a road map to reach unexplored or unacknowledged parts of yourself.

Anger is also a fuel that energizes us to change our lives. What changes has anger precipitated in your life?

3. The sea can also be seen as a metaphor for the unconscious. The man from the sea is a messenger from the unconscious. He represents those restless longings and urges that reach the surface of our minds from time to time. If we ignore them, as the father ignored the man from the sea, we face spiritual hunger, emotional starvation.

For the next three weeks, pay close attention to your dreams and to the thoughts that flit in and out of your consciousness many times a day; look in them for messages from the unconscious. What patterns do you see? What longings, urges, and desires have you been ignoring? What can you do to meet those dreams, needs, and desires?

When we refuse to give our psyche what it needs, it may starve us. Another way to detect unconscious needs is to look at the areas in which we feel emotionally starved or even dead.

Watch yourself closely for areas in which you are shut down. Make a list or map of these areas. Study the list, then put it aside and begin watching for associations and images that come to you, related to these areas. Keep notes. After a week or so, study your notes. Do any of them offer hints of ways in which you could revive yourself, and bring those emotionally malnourished parts of yourself back to life?

Watch closely to discover what situations, people, and inter-

actions nourish your soul. Make a record of those moments when
your heart sings. What patterns do you see?

Make a list of ten things you could do to increase the nourish-
ment to the starved parts of yourself. Choose the two that appeal
to you most, or are easiest to implement, and begin.

Chapter Twenty-four

The Beginning of Wisdom and Law

A Yakima Story

This story describes a battle between two women, who are also mountains, and its aftermath. The defeated woman-mountain, stripped of all her basic attributes, lashes out, causing those around her to suffer. Eventually harmony is restored, and this woman goes on to embody the beginning of wisdom and law.

Long ago, in the days before people were the way they are today, the mountains were women, and the Sun was a man. There was only that one man, though, and there were many women, so they didn't get along very well.

One day, two of the women, Wasco and Pahto, got into a terrible fight. Some say it was because they both loved the Sun and each was jealous of the attention he gave to the other. Others say Wasco was just getting even with Pahto for something that had happened long before.

Either way, Wasco attacked Pahto and knocked off her head. Since Pahto was not just a woman, but also a mountain, that meant that the top of the mountain fell off and broke into pieces, which scattered far and wide across the ground.

Once Wasco had defeated Pahto, she took home all of Pahto's belongings—all the deer, elk, bears, and other animals that lived on her mountainsides, all the salmon and trout and other fish that swam in her streams. All the huckleberries and pine nuts and roots. Everything. By the time Wasco was done, Pahto looked barren and lifeless.

But the injured woman-mountain still had some power left. Without her head, without her usual attributes, she became ugly and cruel. In the summer she sent enormous thunderstorms ripping across the sky and drowned the earth with rain. In the winter she sent snows heavier than any that had fallen before. In the spring she covered the earth with floods.

It was just about then that the new people, our ancestors, appeared. Because of the floods, people couldn't live in the valleys. They couldn't live where the rocks had rolled down from the top because the landscape was too rough. They could only live high on the mountainsides, but there was no food up there, and for much of the year it was cold and uncomfortable.

The Great Maker was watching everything that happened. He watched as Wasco hurried home with all of Pahto's belongings. He watched as the new beings were born, people as we know them today, and he watched as they struggled to survive. He saw that if the new people were to be safe, Pahto must be healed. So the Great Maker returned the salmon and trout and other fish to Pahto's streams. He brought back deer, bears, elk, and other game. He gave Pahto back her huckleberries and herbs, her pine nuts and roots.

Now the new people were much happier. There was plenty of food. Pahto had become a life giver once again.

Still, Pahto lacked a head. So in the place of her fallen peaks, the Great Maker gave Pahto the White Eagle.

At the moment when the White Eagle became her head, Pahto was transformed. She became the law, rising high and white in the sky for all to see. She became the wisest being on earth. She saw the past and knew the future. She watched over the entire world and became the guardian and protector of the people that were to come. And the children of the White Eagle flew far and wide across the earth, bringing back reports of all that happened across the land.

From that day on, the Sun's light came first to Pahto, and she was content. When Wasco saw what had happened, she knew that instead of winning, she had actually lost the battle. She knew there was no point in ever attacking Pahto again.

The two women who were mountains are still standing today. Pahto is that mountain over there, Mount Adams. Wasco is Mount Hood. Even today, Mount Adams is a sacred peak and should not be climbed. Even today, the children of the White Eagle fly far and wide across the earth.

THE WOMAN WHO RULED THE WORLD

 RESEARCH ON ANCIENT SKELETONS HAS produced the controversial finding that non-Indians, sometimes labeled as "Caucasoid," lived in the Americas more than nine thousand years ago. A story of the Okanogan Indians from the Plateau region supports that hypothesis.

Long ago the whole world consisted of a single island in the middle of the ocean, named White Man's Island. White giants lived there. Their leader was a woman named Scomalt. Some say she created the world. Others say she merely ruled it.

For many years the white giants lived peacefully. But eventually they began to quarrel. Scomalt asked them to stop, but they wouldn't. When their fighting got so bad she couldn't stand it anymore, she made them all gather at one end of the island. Then she broke that piece of the island off from the rest and sent it floating away.

Storms battered the little fragment of floating land so badly that only one man and one woman survived. By the time they reached the main island again, they were so sunburned they were no longer white; they were brown. By then, Scomalt had retreated to her own private place. The man and woman settled in Okanogan country and became the grandmother and grandfather of the People.

CONNECTING THE STORY TO YOUR LIFE

1. The low point in Pahto's life comes when she loses not only her head, but all the other qualities that make her most uniquely herself. Completely stripped of everything that is the essence of who she is, she turns mean and vicious.

Have there been points in your life when you lost your sense of who you are? How did you act? What helped you regain your sense of self?

2. As this story illustrates, there can be no wisdom and law without having first gone through the torture of transformation. Write a poem, paint a picture, or create a narrative that uses incidents from your own life to illustrate this idea.

3. Metaphorically, the eagle that causes Pahto to become the beginning of law represents the joining of earth and sky. This reflects the idea that the basic laws of human behavior arise at the point where two related elements touch: love and hate, light and dark, life and death, relationship and solitude, sickness and health.

If you tend to think in these terms, sit down and write out five basic laws of human behavior that you have observed in yourself and others over the years. What do they mean to you? How do they operate in your life or affect your life?

If you'd prefer to be less analytical, do a sand painting or create a display on your shrine that relates to your feelings and reactions to this story.

Chapter Twenty-five

Dancing for Nomtaimet

A Tale from the Wintu People

Few stories in any tradition around the world celebrate the joy in womanhood more vividly than this tale from central California.

The girl named Nomtaimet reached the age of becoming a woman. Although this happened long ago, the world was already much the way it is today, with the rivers flowing into the sea.

Nomtaimet and her family lived in a village that was already old. Everything was as it had always been, since the day the first humans appeared. Women ground acorns with pestles. They cooked by heating stones and dropping them into the water in special baskets. Men fished. They hunted with snares and bows and arrows.

Nomtaimet's parents were careful people. They respected their ancestors and the customs that had been passed down since the beginning of time. So when Nomtaimet became a woman, her mother built a little house for her, not too far from her family home. There the girl, who was now a young woman, went to live by herself for many moons, as was the custom. All day she sat alone in her hut. The only people she saw were her mother and her mother's mother. They washed her and brushed her hair. They brought her meals and took care of her in every way, for during this time in a woman's life, she does not take care of herself, but only sits and ponders, or prays, and listens to all that her mother and her mother's mother tell her about what it means to be a woman.

Nomtaimet did well. She learned everything her mother and her mother's mother taught her. She prayed. She pondered. She ate. She fasted. She did all that a young woman does, according to the rituals of the ancestors.

Finally, when the winds of winter passed, and the new clover sprouted across the earth in the springtime, Nomtaimet's period of separation ended.

As always happens, the young woman emerged from this time of solitude more beautiful than ever.

Everyone in her family—her father and her mother, her father's mother and her father's father, her mother's mother and her mother's father, and all their brothers and sisters—pitched in and gave a party to honor Nomtaimet. They invited everyone in the village. They sent messages to all the people living in other villages to come and join them. The women pounded acorns. They heated rocks and dropped them into the water in the cooking baskets and cooked all kinds of wonderful dishes.

Nomtaimet was dressed in the most beautiful clothes imaginable. She wore a new buckskin skirt decorated with shells and beads. She wore so many shiny new necklaces that they covered half her chest. Mink ties held her long black braids in place. In her hands she carried fine rattles made from deer hooves.

Everyone stood around and admired Nomtaimet's beauty. The young married women from the village presented her with a new willow staff to honor her womanhood.

Finally someone said, "It's time to do the circle dance." Since the beginning of the world, this dance has honored the moment when a girl becomes a woman.

The old men and women resting inside their huts heard the sound of the feet shuffling from side to side and came out to join the dance. The children heard the singing. They heard the sound of feet pounding up and down. They stopped their games and came running to join in. Even the women who were cooking put down their tools and danced.

Soon the whole village was dancing an enormous circle dance. The earth shook as the people sang and circled, circled and sang, stamping and shuffling their feet.

Then people arrived from other villages, and it was time for the great feast.

For ten days and ten nights the villagers and their guests sang and danced and ate, ate and danced and sang in honor of Nomtaimet.

The feast came to an end. Everyone said it was the best feast any young woman had ever had, and what a wonderful young woman Nomtaimet was, and what a fine life she would have.

Then, instead of going home, as they normally would have, people kept on dancing. They danced and danced and danced.

They formed a line and danced their way up the trail that led out of the village to the east. They danced over rocks. They danced through the bushes. They danced along the riverbanks. They danced up and down the hills.

They danced along the ridge tops. They danced past the springs. They danced through streams.

They danced so long that their clothes fell off. They painted their bodies and their faces, and kept right on dancing.

They danced through the deserts and they danced across the mountains. They danced through the plains and they danced through the forests. They danced through the marshes and they danced along the seashore.

They danced through the springtime and they danced through the summer. They danced through the autumn and they danced through the winter.

They danced all around the world. Just as the winter winds ended and the clover covered the earth with fresh green leaves, they arrived back at their village.

Now the dance ended. People made themselves new clothes and went back to their old lives. But no one ever forgot the seasons of dancing for Nomtaimet. And today, when a girl becomes a young woman, she learns the story of Nomtaimet, whose womanhood was honored by a dance that stretched all across the world.

WHITE PAINTED WOMAN

 EVEN TODAY SOME NATIVE AMERICAN
peoples preserve the custom of honoring a
girl's transition to womanhood. In the Southwest, Navajo medicine
women still perform puberty ceremonies for young women, following their first period. The ceremonies are shorter and the tasks the
young woman must perform are less rigorous. But ancient songs and
rituals remain.

Similarly, Apaches, who are cultural and linguistic cousins of the
Navajos, preserve puberty rites. These include an ancient song in
honor of White Painted Woman.

> White Painted Woman,
> I come to you
> By the power of the life you give me,
> I come to you
> By the power of the blessings you give me,
> I come to you
> By the power of the good fortune you grant me,
> I come to you
> By all your many fruits,
> I come to you
> Throughout a long life,
> I will come to you.
> By the power of these holy truths,
> You move across the earth.

SONG OF REJOICING

FEW STORIES CELEBRATE WOMANHOOD AS joyously and elaborately as "Dancing for Nomtaimet," but most traditions include various forms of celebration. Women among the Pawnee of the Great Plains sang this song of rejoicing. Like some other traditional songs from many Native American cultures, the syllables have no literal meaning, but are meant to convey a mood, in this case joy.

> *Ya e-e yo ah o*
> *ah o e-e-e-e-e he ya!*
> *He e ah he-e ya*
> *He a ah he-e ya*
> *Ha-o ha he ah ha-e ya*
> *Ha-o ho-o wi ya ha i ya!*

CONNECTING THE STORY TO YOUR LIFE

1. Think back to the time of your first menstruation and all that went with it. How did your mother act, your father, your siblings? Was it a secret, or was it something everyone talked about? Were there parts of the experience that made you feel honored, parts of it that made you feel shamed?

If you could redo all this, what would you do differently, or how would you have others act differently?

Create a mythic narrative about your puberty experience. Or do a visualization in which you imagine yourself going through the kind of sacred, meditative transition to womanhood that Nomtaimet underwent, a ritual that honors you as you come into your power.

2. In this story it is a given that Nomtaimet's solitude and contemplation make her even more beautiful. This relates to the idea that when you reach the essence of who and what you are, free of illusion, it makes you more beautiful than ever.

What periods of solitude have you undergone in your own life? How have they been transforming? How have they helped you get in touch with your core self?

3. If you are already a dancer, next time you dance, dance in Nomtaimet's honor. Dance in honor of yourself. Dance in honor of women everywhere.

If you do not dance, do a visualization in which you imagine yourself dancing in Nomtaimet's honor, in your own honor, and in honor of all women on earth. What feelings, memories, dreams, or other associations does this visualization bring up for you?

4. Create a song of rejoicing to celebrate yourself, your womanhood, your connection to all women, present, future, and past.

5. Plan to make the next twelve months a year of celebration. Plan one event a day, or one event a week, even if it lasts only five minutes a day, or half an hour a week. These are your moments of glory. These are your moments of celebrating yourself for who you are.

Afterword

If you've worked through the exercises, save all your writings, tapes, paintings, and other creations. On the calendar, set aside a day six months from now to look back over everything. On that day write down emotions, ideas, and images that occur to you as you review what you've done.

If you enjoyed using a shrine, keep the shrine in place. Change the items you feature on it to match your changing experiences, moods, dreams.

Write a letter to the self you expect to be five years from now. Date it, sign it, seal it. Put it in some safe place where you will be able to find it easily.

Casting yourself as the central character, create one final narrative of your life in a style that could be passed on through oral tradition from generation to generation.

Make a date with yourself, once a month, during the season when spiders are out, to sit quietly and look at a spiderweb until you begin feeling some stirring of inner voice or wisdom. Or simply listen for the wind, the messenger of Spider Woman, to bring the answers or advice you seek.

May the spirit of Spider Woman, White Buffalo Woman, Nomtaimet, and all the other ancient Women of Power stay with you.

May they protect you and guide you. May they encourage you and give you faith in yourself. May they help you feel connected with all those who have gone before. May your life become a dance of joy that celebrates your womanhood, your personhood, yourself.

Acknowledgments

Navajo storytellers Ruth Roessel and her sisters and Tohono O'odham storytellers Regina Siquieros and Mary Bernice Belin gave me invaluable insights into Native American traditions related to women and storytelling. Other Native Americans who have contributed to my understanding of storytelling and other traditions include Danny Lopez, Edith Franklin, Stella Tucker, Monty Roessel, Anita and Joseph Suazo, Herbert and Ben Yates, Karen Denilaikai, Shannon McKenna, Denise Perez, Cloud Eagle, Mary Yazzie Sampson, Harold Kenton, Dominic Arquero, and Imogene Goodshot.

Native American writers who have influenced my thought and writing most strongly include Vine Deloria, Jr., Alfonso Ortiz, Leslie Marmon Silko, N. Scott Momaday, and Paula Gunn Allen.

Laura Holt of the Museum of New Mexico's Laboratory of Anthropology helped me obtain early versions of the stories presented here.

William and Beth Hammond, Susan Arritt, Angela and Karl Storch, Elena and Flavio Garcia, Schia Muterperl, Mary Cable, Ken Macrorie, Eduardo Fuss, Judy Gordon, Judy Roberts, Iska Sargent, Barbara Murphy, Paul Golding and above all Kenneth Duerre nurtured and encouraged me while I worked on this book.

The faith of my editor, Sheila Curry, brought this book into existence. Then Sheila Moody did a fine job of copyediting.

My deepest thanks to each of you.

For Further Reading

The following list of suggested readings includes books related to both the stories and the supplemental questions. The list is meant to serve as a springboard to further resources for those who have a general interest in the subject.

Scholars and serious students of folklore will want to go to the multivolume *Report of the Bureau of American Ethnology* and to the *Journal of American Folklore,* especially from 1890–1910. See also the outstanding bibliography in Stith Thompson's *Tales of the North American Indian.*

In Native American languages, traditional storytelling is typically repetitive, elliptic, and full of allusions. For a superb rendering of this, see Leanne Hinton and Lucille J. Watahomigie's *Spirit Mountain: An Anthology of Yuman Story and Song.*

For a more detailed list of works consulted by the author in researching and writing *Spider Woman's Web,* write to P.O. Box 8400, Santa Fe, NM 87504-8400. Enclose a self-addressed 9"x12" manila envelope stamped with $3.20 postage, plus $5.00 to cover handling and copying costs.

Ackerman, Lillian, ed. *A Song to the Creator: Traditional Arts of Native American Women of the Plateau.* Norman: University of Oklahoma Press, 1996.

Adamson, Thelma, ed. *Folk-Tales of the Coast Salish.* New York: American Folklore Society, 1934.

Allen, Paula Gunn. *Grandmothers of the Light: A Medicine Woman's Sourcebook.* Boston: Beacon Press, 1991.

———. *The Sacred Hoop: Recovering the Feminine in American Indian Traditions.* Boston: Beacon Press, 1992.

Astrov, Margot, ed. *American Indian Prose and Poetry.* Boston: Beacon Press, 1992.

Awiakta, Marilou. *Selu: Seeking the Corn-Mother's Wisdom.* Golden, Colo.: Fulcrum, 1993.

Bass, Ellen, and Laura Davis. *The Courage to Heal: A Guide for Woman Survivors of Child Sexual Abuse,* 3rd edition. New York: HarperCollins, 1994.

Boas, Franz. *Folktales of Salishan and Sehaptin Tribes.* Lancaster, Pa.: American Folklore Society, 1917.

Bradshaw, John. *Family Secrets: The Path to Self-Acceptance and Reunion.* New York: Bantam, 1996.

Bramson, Robert M. *Coping with Difficult People.* New York: Dell, 1988.

Brown, Joseph Epes, ed. *The Sacred Pipe: Black Elk's Account of the Seven Rites of the Oglala Sioux.* New York: Penguin, 1971.

Bruchac, Joseph. *Lasting Echoes: An Oral History of Native American People.* New York: Harcourt Brace, 1997.

———. *The Native American Sweat Lodge: History and Legends.* Freedom, Calif.: The Crossing Press, 1993.

Buchanan, Kimberly Moore. *Apache Women Warriors,* 2nd edition. El Paso: University of Texas Press, 1996.

Cahill, Susan, ed. *Wise Women: Over Two Thousand Years of Spiritual Writing by Women.* New York: Norton, 1996.

Cameron, Julia. *The Artist's Way.* New York: Putnam, 1992.

———. *The Vein of Gold: A Journey to Your Creative Heart.* New York: Putnam, 1996.

Chinen, A. B., M.D. *Waking the World: Classic Tales of Women and the Heroic Feminine.* New York: Tarcher, 1996.

Clark, Ella E. *Indian Legends from the Northern Rockies.* Norman: University of Oklahoma Press, 1988.

———. *Indian Legends of the Pacific Northwest.* Berkeley: University of California Press, 1969.

Coffin, Tristram P., ed. *Indian Tales of North America.* Philadelphia: American Folklore Society, 1961.

Courlander, Harold. *Hopi Voices: Recollections, Traditions, and Narratives of the Hopi Indians.* Albuquerque: University of New Mexico Press, 1982.

Crow Dog, Mary, and Richard Erdoes. *Lakota Woman.* New York: HarperCollins, 1990.

Crowell, Al. *I'd Rather Be Married.* Oakland, Calif.: New Harbinger, 1995.

Curtis, Edward S. *The North American Indian, Being a Series of Volumes Picturing and Describing the Indians of the United States and Alaska,* edited by Frederick Webb Hodge. New York: Johnson Reprint Corporation, 1907.

Curtis, Natalie. *The Indians' Book: An Offering by the American Indians of Indian Lore. . . .* New York: Harper's, 1907.

Davis, Mary B., ed. *Native America in the Twentieth Century: An Encyclopedia.* New York: Garland, 1994.

DeHuff, Elizabeth Willis. *Taytay's Tales: Collected and Retold.* New York: Harcourt Brace, 1922.

Deloria, Vine, Jr. *God Is Red: A Native View of Religion,* 2nd edition. Golden, Colo.: Fulcrum, 1994.

Derounian-Stodola, Kathryn Zabelle, ed. *Women's Indian Captivity Narratives.* New York: Penguin, 1998.

Dodge, Robert K., and Joseph B. McCullough, eds. *New and Old Voices of Wah'kon-tah.* New York: International Publishers, 1985.

Donovan, Kathleen M. *Feminist Readings of Native American Literature: Coming to Voice.* Tucson: University of Arizona Press, 1998.

Erdoes, Richard, Ed. *The Sound of Flutes and Other Indian Legends.* New York: Pantheon, 1976.

————, and Alfonso Ortiz, eds. *American Indian Myths and Legends.* New York: Pantheon, 1985.

Estés, Clarissa Pinkola. *The Dangerous Old Woman: Myths and Stories of the Wise Old Woman Archetype.* New York: Random House, 1997.

————. *Women Who Run with the Wolves.* New York: Ballantine, 1992.

Faraday, Ann. *Dr. Ann Faraday's Dream Power.* New York: Berkley, 1997.

Farmer, Steven. *Adult Children of Abusive Parents.* New York: Ballantine, 1990.

Forward, Susan. *Toxic Parents: Overcoming Their Hurtful Legacy and Reclaiming Your Life.* New York: Bantam, 1989.

Frisbie, Charlotte Johnson. *Kinaaldá: A Study of the Navaho Girl's Puberty Ceremony.* Salt Lake City: University of Utah Press, 1993.

Garfield, Patricia. *The Dream Messenger*. New York: Simon & Schuster, 1997.

———. *The Healing Power of Dreams*. New York: Simon & Schuster, 1992.

Garrett, Michael. *Walking on the Wind: Cherokee Teachings for Harmony and Balance*. Santa Fe, N.M.: Bear and Company, 1998.

Gottman, John. *Why Marriages Succeed or Fail*. New York: Simon & Schuster, 1994.

Greer, Mary K. *Women of the Golden Dawn: Rebels and Priestesses*. Rochester, Vt.: Park Street Press, 1995.

Grinnell, George Bird. *Blackfoot Lodge Tales: The Story of a Prairie People*. Lincoln: University of Nebraska Press, 1962.

———. *By Cheyenne Campfires*. Lincoln: University of Nebraska Press, 1971.

Gunn, John M. *Schat-chen: History, Traditions and Narratives of the Queres Indians of Laguna and Acoma*. Albuquerque, N.M.: Albright and Anderson, 1917.

Hale, Janet Campbell. *Bloodlines: Odyssey of a Native Daughter*. Tucson: University of Arizona Press, 1993.

Hazen-Hammond, Susan. *Timelines of Native American History*. New York: Berkley, 1997.

Hendrix, Harville. *Getting the Love You Want: A Guide for Couples*. New York: HarperCollins, 1990.

———. *Keeping the Love You Find: A Guide for Singles*. New York: Simon & Schuster, 1992.

Hinton, Leanne, and Lucille J. Watahomigie, eds. *Spirit Mountain: An Anthology of Yuman Story and Song*. Tucson: Sun Tracks and the University of Arizona Press, 1984.

Hogan, Linda, et al., eds. *Intimate Nature: The Bond Between Women and Animals*. New York: Ballantine, 1998.

Iglehart, Hallie. *Womanspirit: A Guide to Women's Wisdom*. New York: HarperCollins, 1983.

Johnson, Dorothy M. *Buffalo Woman*. Lincoln: University of Nebraska Press, 1995.

Jung, C. G. *Dreams*. New York: Fine Communications, 1996.

Jung, Carl G., et al. *Man and His Symbols*. New York: Doubleday, 1969.

Kroeber, Theodora. *The Inland Whale*. Bloomington: Indiana University Press, 1959.

Kübler-Ross, Elisabeth. *Death: The Final Stage of Growth.* New York: Simon & Schuster, 1986.

———. *On Death and Dying.* New York: Simon & Schuster, 1997.

LaBerge, Stephen. *Lucid Dreaming.* New York: Ballantine, 1986.

Leland, Charles G. *The Algonquin Legends of New England.* Mineola, N.Y.: Dover, 1992.

Locke, Raymond Friday. *The Book of the Navajo,* 5th edition. Los Angeles: Mankind Publishing Company, 1992.

Lummis, Charles. *Pueblo Indian Folk-Stories.* Lincoln: University of Nebraska Press, 1992.

Maltz, Wendy. *The Sexual Healing Journey: A Guide for Survivors of Sexual Abuse.* New York: HarperCollins, 1992.

Maslow, Abraham H. *Toward a Psychology of Being,* 3rd edition. New York: Wiley, 1998.

Miller, Alice. *Prisoners of Childhood.* New York: Basic, 1996.

———. *Thou Shalt Not Be Aware: Society's Betrayal of the Child.* New York: Farrar, Straus and Giroux, 1998.

Momaday, N. Scott. *The Way to Rainy Mountain.* Albuquerque: University of New Mexico Press, 1969.

Moore, Thomas. *Care of the Soul: A Guide for Cultivating Depth and Sacredness in Everyday Life.* New York: HarperCollins, 1992.

———. *The Soul of Sex: Cultivating Life as an Act of Love.* New York: HarperCollins, 1998.

Mullett, G. M. *Spider Woman Stories: Legends of the Hopi Indians.* Tucson: University of Arizona Press, 1979.

Murdock, Maureen. *The Heroine's Journey.* Boston: Shambhala, 1990.

Neihardt, John G. *Black Elk Speaks: Being the Life Story of a Holy Man of the Oglala Sioux.* Lincoln: University of Nebraska Press, 1979.

———. *The Sixth Grandfather: Black Elk's Teachings Given to John G. Neihardt,* edited by Raymond J. DeMallie. Lincoln: University of Nebraska Press, 1985.

Niethammer, Carolyn. *Daughters of the Earth: The Lives and Legends of American Indian Women.* New York: Simon & Schuster, 1996.

Null, Gary. *Secrets of the Sacred White Buffalo.* Paramus, N.J.: Prentice-Hall, 1998.

Opler, Morris Edward. *An Apache Life-Way: The Economic, Social, and Reli-*

gious Institutions of the Chiricahua Indians. Lincoln: University of Nebraska Press, 1996.

Ortiz, Alfonso. *The Tewa World: Space, Time, Being, and Becoming in a Pueblo Society.* Chicago: University of Chicago Press, 1972.

Parsons, Elsie Clews. *Tewa Tales.* Tucson: University of Arizona Press, 1994.

————. *Taos Tales.* Mineola, N.Y.: Dover, 1996.

Patterson-Rudolph, Carol. *On the Trail of Spider Woman: Petroglyphs, Pictographs, and Myths of the Southwest.* Santa Fe, N.M.: Ancient City Press, 1997.

Perdue, Theda. *Cherokee Women: Gender and Culture Change 1700–1835.* Lincoln: University of Nebraska Press, 1998.

Peterson, Scott. *Native American Prophecies: Examining the History, Wisdom, and Startling Predictions of Visionary Native Americans.* St. Paul, Minn.: Paragon House, 1990.

Pipher, Mary. *Reviving Ophelia.* New York: Ballantine, 1994.

Prucha, Francis Paul. *Atlas of American Indian Affairs.* Lincoln and London: University of Nebraska Press, 1990.

Radin, Paul. *Winnebago Culture as Described by Themselves.* Baltimore; Waverly Press, 1950.

Reuss, Frederick J. *Saynday Was Coming Along.* Washington, D.C.: Smithsonian Institution, 1993.

Rice, Julian. *Black Elk's Story: Distinguishing Its Lakota Purpose.* Albuquerque: University of New Mexico Press, 1994.

————. *Deer Women and Elk Men: The Lakota Narratives of Ella Deloria.* Albuquerque: University of New Mexico Press, 1992.

Roessel, Ruth. *Women in Navajo Society.* Rough Rock, Navajo Nation: Navajo Resource Center, Rough Rock Demonstration School, 1981.

Rothenberg, Jerome, comp. *Shaking the Pumpkin: Traditional Poetry of the Indian North Americas,* revised edition. Albuquerque: University of New Mexico Press, 1991.

Schoolcraft, Henry Rowe. *Schoolcraft's Indian Legends,* edited by Mentor L. Williams. Michigan State University, 1956.

Sevillano, Mando. *The Hopi Way: Tales from a Vanishing Culture.* Flagstaff, Ariz.: Northland Press, 1986.

Silko, Leslie Marmon. *Storyteller.* New York: Arcade, 1981.

Smith, Ann W. *Grandchildren of Alcoholics: Another Generation of Co-Dependency.* Deerfield Beach, Fla.: Health Communications, 1988.

Spier, Leslie. *Yuman Tribes of the Gila River.* Mineola, N.Y.: Dover, 1978.

St. Pierre, Mark, and Tilda Long Soldier. *Walking in the Sacred Manner: Healers, Dreamers, and Pipe Carriers—Medicine Women of the Plains Indians.* New York: Simon & Schuster, 1995.

Sumrall, Amber Coverdale, and Patrice Vecchione, eds. *Storming Heaven's Gate: An Anthology of Spiritual Writings by Women.* New York: Penguin, 1997.

Tannen, Deborah. *That's Not What I Meant: How Conversational Style Makes or Breaks Relationships.* New York: Ballantine, 1987.

Thompson, Stith. *Tales of North American Indians.* Bloomington: Indiana University Press, 1966.

Turner, Frederick, ed. *The Portable North American Indian Reader.* New York: Penguin, 1977.

Walker, Barbara G. *The Crone: Woman of Age, Wisdom, and Power.* New York: HarperCollins, 1985.

———. *The Woman's Encyclopedia of Myths and Secrets.* New York: HarperCollins, 1983.

Weenoocheeyoo peesaduehnee yak:anup—Stories of Our Ancestors: A Collection of Northern-Ute Indian Tales. Salt Lake City, Utah: Uintah-Ouray Ute Tribe, 1974.

Woodman, Marion. *Dancing in the Flames: The Dark Goddess in the Transformation of Consciousness.* Boston: Shambhala, 1997.

———, et al. *Leaving My Father's House: A Journey to Conscious Femininity.* Boston: Shambhala, 1993.

Zitkala-Sa. *American Indian Stories.* Lincoln: University of Nebraska Press, 1985.

———. *Old Indian Legends.* Lincoln: University of Nebraska Press, 1985.

Zolbrod, Paul G. *Diné bahanè: The Navajo Creation Story.* Albuquerque: University of New Mexico Press, 1984.

Index

About the Author

Susan Hazen-Hammond is the author of nine nonfiction books. These include two other books on Native Americans, *Timelines of Native American History*, which was selected as an alternate by the Quality Paperback Book Club, and a new children's book from Dutton, *Thunder Bear and Ko: The Buffalo Nation and Nambe Pueblo*. Her other books include *Chile Pepper Fever: Mine's Hotter Than Yours*; *The Great Saguaro Book*; and a forthcoming book of true stories from history, *Into the Unknown*. She has also written more than three hundred articles, poems, reviews, and short stories, including accounts of her experiences among Native Americans in the United States and beyond.

Before moving to New Mexico in 1980, Hazen-Hammond taught psychology at Peninsula College in Port Angeles, Washington. She has also studied folklore and has long been deeply interested both in women's studies and in the healing power of traditional Native American stories.

Hazen-Hammond comes from a long line of New Englanders. Her ancestors include Abenaki men and women. In addition to writing, she is a painter and award-winning photographer.

About the Covers

For thousands of years, Native Americans have painted sacred symbols on stone, wood, metal, and clay. They have woven them into baskets and clothing, pecked them into rock faces, carved them into wood, buried them with their dead.

Many ancient symbols survive. For the front cover, our designer has chosen the power-filled mountain turkey, from the Keresan-speaking Pueblo Indians of the Southwest. Just as the eagle represents the sky, the mountain turkey represents the earth. The turkey links present with past and future. It accompanies and guides human beings through life, and into death. It carries messages between humans and the spirits.

When the first Europeans appeared, in the early 1500s, the People gave them gifts of turkeys and turkey feathers.

Today, farther west and south, every autumn as the air grows colder, storytellers among the Tohono O'odham peoples of the Sonoran Desert wait and watch for the moment when rattlesnakes retreat underground. On that day, winter begins, and with it, the season of telling stories.

On the back cover is a photograph of Tohono O'odham storyteller Regina Siquieros, who tells the story of a young woman who disappears into the earth and reappears as a symbol of strength and power, in the form of the first saguaro cactus.